Basic Skills for Childcare – Literacy

Tutor Pack

Excellence in Childcare
Series Editor: Maureen Smith

This book is part of the Excellence in Childcare series. The series is designed to support students and NVQ candidates, practitioners, managers and trainers to develop their skills and offer a high quality service to children and families.

Books in the series are written by experts with many years' experience of and commitment to the childcare sector. As the sector grows and develops, there is a demand not only for more childcare provision, but for better quality provision. The sector now requires very well qualified, excellent practitioners who can support children's development throughout the preschool years. The series aims to help new and established practitioners become confident, imaginative, excellent professionals.

Basic Skills for Childcare – Literacy

Tutor Pack

June Green

David Fulton Publishers

MT

David Fulton Publishers Ltd
The Chiswick Centre, 414 Chiswick High Road, London W4 5TF

www.fultonpublishers.co.uk

David Fulton Publishers is a division of Granada Learning Limited, part of the Granada Media group.

First published in Great Britain by David Fulton Publishers 2003

10 9 8 7 6 5 4 3 2 1

British Library Cataloguing in Publication Data
A catalogue record for this book is available from the British Library.

ISBN 1-84312-021-6

Typeset by FiSH Books, London
Printed and bound in Great Britain by Ashford Colour Press Limited, Gosport, Hants

3/21/04

Contents

Acknowledgements

I would like to thank the following people, without whom this book would never have been written:

Steve Lee – my star among stars – who deserves special thanks; Trish Jacobs whose wacky sense of humour kept me going and who I'm glad I sit next to; Gail Blackwood – proof-reader extraordinaire – for her unflappable calmness and valued suggestions.

My thanks also to Ruth Lane – the holder of many hidden talents – who saved me when all came crashing down; staff in IT, who were so patient and helpful; my CAHCE DCE group 2001–2003, for letting me use their names, for taking an interest and encouraging me, and for giving me a day off; staff in the Early Childhood Studies, Care and Public Services Department at South Birmingham College, for their enthusiasm and encouragement; Nina Stibbe, of David Fulton Publishers, who gave me an opportunity I never dreamed of and whose endless support, encouragement and good humour makes her one of the nicest people I know.

There are countless others I ought to thank, but I fear I would end up writing another book. Right now, I would like to get a life for a while!

You know who you are and I thank you.

June Green
South Birmingham College
February 2003

Dedicated to my son, Radley
for all the support and encouragement, despite
the late and missed meals.
I couldn't have done it without you.

An Introduction to the Resource File

Welcome to Basic Skills Literacy for childcare

As a busy childcare and education tutor, with a full timetable, the last thing you want to be landed with is preparing a whole lot of Basic Skills lessons. Why? Because it means more planning, more research and more valuable time spent finding resources. Where on earth are you expected to find the time to do it all?

I have been there and have certainly learnt a lot along the way. This *Basic Skills For Childcare – Literacy (Tutor Pack)* is largely a result of my own experience of the day-to-day pressures that teachers face. If Basic Skills Literacy has been added to your teaching responsibilities, this book is for you.

The pack contains all the materials you need to take you through Basic Skills Literacy from Entry Level One to Level Two. It starts with a preliminary session that is designed to introduce Basic Skills to students at all levels. The remaining chapters deal with each level in turn and follow a similar format. Each chapter comprises a handful of sessions, whose basic framework is as follows:

- General introduction to the level and its contents.
- Session outline – each one starts by telling you what resources you will need for that session (e.g. newspapers, dictionaries, etc.) and sets out the focus of the session, enabling you to plan ahead.
- Activities – all of which are broken down into various steps and based mainly around childcare, particularly in the later levels, which makes them relevant to students' lives. Wherever possible, relevant Basic Skills criteria have been matched to the activities and referenced in the margin.
- Handouts/Activity Sheets – ready to be photocopied.

Sessions are based on two- to three-hour stints, but they can easily be separated if you are short of time, and are thoroughly interchangeable so that different activities can be chosen and combined to suit your own particular needs. You can start anywhere within the levels and it is quite easy to 'pick and mix' the activities from different levels if you have a mixed-ability group – differentiation covered!

Some words of advice before you begin

➤ The accompanying Students' Workbook contains spelling quizzes, a section on spelling rules, space for keeping a dictionary of their own, and various other things that students are likely to need to be able to work and develop independently. There are supplementary activities which students can work on either at home or in class if they finish set activities before their classmates. It makes sense for every student to have their own copy of the workbook.

➤ Start collecting magazines, newspapers, leaflets, TV guides, telephone directories, etc. You will use lots of them!

➤ Have a dictionary available for every individual student. School dictionaries are good to work with at the lower levels, but by the time students reach later levels they need access to more comprehensive dictionaries and thesauruses.

With regards to the Speaking and Listening sections of Basic Skills, the sessions included in this pack provide numerous opportunities for covering a lot of these skills, through discussions, paired activities, reading work and so on. In addition to this, at the end of each level you will find some activities that specifically cover Speaking and Listening. You might want to use these as assessment material, or as a basis for teaching the Speaking and Listening skills. Alternatively, they will act as supplementary activities that can be built into your regular sessions.

What I will say is this: it is crucial that Speaking and Listening is seen as being equally important as reading and writing. In any vocation, good communication skills are important. In childcare, they are even more so. As adults working with children, students and childcare workers are role models whom children will imitate and learn from. We cannot expect children to be able to communicate well if the adults around them do not show them how to speak and listen effectively.

I hope you find this pack useful and that, above all, you and your students will have fun with it.

CHAPTER 1

Introductory Session

Introducing the Basic Skills

This needs to be a light, fun session. What you do here will almost certainly set the tone for the rest of the course, so try not to let things get too heavy. The session is made up of six activities.

Activity 1   What are the Basic Skills?

Give out copies of Handout 1, 'What are Basic Skills?' and go through it with the students.

Activity 2   Explanation

Examine the different areas that make up Basic Skills Literacy:

* Give each student a copy of Handout 2, 'Basic Skills Literacy' and go through it together.
* Explain that this is what you will be covering in the forthcoming sessions. Students will progress through the levels, gaining new skills and developing those they already have. There will be lots of activities, quizzes and games along the way.

Activity 3   When will I need to use these skills?

* Use this question as the basis for a group discussion and follow with an exercise in which students list their own suggestions, using Handout 3, 'When will I need to use these skills?' as a starting point.
* Give the students an opportunity to feed back and discuss the ideas they generated during the activity.

Activity 4   Reflection

* Invite the students to reflect on the following:
* What are their feelings so far?
* How do they feel about spending a few hours a week on this?
* Can they see the need for it?
* Do they want to do it? Why/why not?

Activity 5   Discussion

Spend some time together working on an 'Improving my literacy skills will...' activity. See how many suggestions the students can come up with.

Activity 6 Explanation

End by giving your students general information about what they will be covering in Basic Skills sessions and how it links to the students' Basic Skills screening results from their induction screening. Finally, give out the students' workbooks and explain what they contain and how they are to be used.

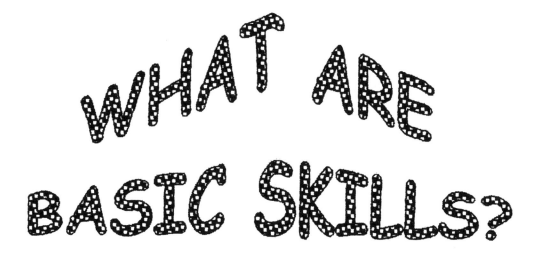

'The ability to read, write and speak English at a level to function and progress at work and in society in general.'

Basic Skills Agency

Basic Skills Literacy

READING

❖ Using different techniques

❖ The meaning and uses of different texts

❖ How to find information

❖ Identifying main points from text

WRITING

❖ Spelling

❖ Punctuation

❖ Grammar

❖ Constructing writing

SPEAKING AND LISTENING

❖ Listening and responding

❖ Communicating

❖ Engaging in discussion

When will I need to use these skills?

Think about the times you will need to use your literacy skills. Some examples have been filled in for you below. Try and think of some more.

	PERSONAL LIFE	COURSEWORK	PLACEMENT
READING	Cooking instructions	Textbooks	Fire evacuation instructions
WRITING	Text messages	Assignments	For children to copy
SPEAKING AND LISTENING	Phone calls	Class discussions	Reading to children

There are lots of times when these skills come in useful, aren't there?

CHAPTER 2

Entry Level One

Introduction

Before we do anything we need to know that the learners understand the basics of reading and writing. Teaching someone how to spell, punctuate, etc. is of no use if they do not understand the basic mechanics. The sessions in this level provide a series of activities that are designed to reinforce these fundamental skills. You may not need to spend much time on this but it does need to be done.

SESSION 1

Outline

This session will take the learner through the basic mechanics of reading and writing. It will give you the chance to gauge confidence and encourage the more reluctant learners.

> For this session you will need:
>
> - Postcards for each student, on which the following should be written:
>
>   My name is ....
>
>   I live in .... (street name and town only).
>
>   I am .... years old.
>
>   I am doing the .... course at .... college.

Activities

Activity 1 Introduction

Introduce the session by explaining to learners that a part of Basic Skills involves reading and writing. Tell them that they will be learning about spelling, decoding words, punctuation, reading and writing different text types, and so on. Point out that before they begin to learn all this, it is important to make sure the basic mechanisms are in place.

Discuss ideas on why we need to know how to read and write, and list suggestions on a flipchart. Tie in with this the fact that a great deal of our time, especially when doing a course, is spent reading and writing.

Examine ways in which we take in and give out much information through reading and writing.

Activity 2   Group discussion – What is reading?

Points to make:

- Reading is what we are doing when we look at something someone else has written and we take meaning from it.
- Write the following example on the flipchart/board: 'Your next tutorial is at 10 a.m. on the 24th January.' This means that you have to meet with your tutor at that time on that date for a tutorial.
- All words have meaning. When these words are put together they form text.
- When you read these words, you are receiving a message or information that has been written by someone else.

Activity 3   Explanation

Points to make:

- When we read in English we read from the left of the page to the right and from the top of the page to the bottom.
- Whatever we are reading, we read it like this.
- It will have been written like this so that it makes sense when read this way.

Activity 4   Focus exercise

Give out copies of Handout 4, 'Reading in English' and go through it with the students, reinforcing what you have already explained. When you have done this, give each student a copy of Activity Sheet 1, 'Different sorts of texts' and see if they can identify the various examples shown.

Activity 5   Focus exercise

When you have gone through the handout, give out the postcards and, working in pairs, ask learners to follow the text and read it to their partner. As learners are reading, go around the room and make sure that they are able to follow the text and to read it. It is important to let learners know that if they can't recognise a word at this stage it doesn't matter. The object of this activity is to put the mechanics of reading into place.

Activity 6   Group discussion – What is writing?

Points to make:

- Writing is a more permanent way of using language than speaking.
- It involves the formation of letters, which are put together to make words.
- Words are then set out on paper in a way that gives meaning to the reader.
- Writing is a way of making a record of something, passing on information and storing something we do not want to forget.

For example:

During your course a lot of people will be talking to you and giving you information – tutors, lecturers, nursery nurses, mentors, your fellow students. You can't keep it all in your head. With a million and one other things on your mind you're bound to forget something important.

Imagine missing an important homework deadline because you didn't write it down and that romantic date with your partner pushed it clean out of your mind!

Another example:

In childcare, lots of records and information are kept about the children. Some of it is basic information such as name, address, and so on.

Activity 7   Discussion/idea storm

Can students suggest what other information/records about the children might need to be kept in a written format? These might include the following:

Parental responsibility   Contact telephone number
Allergies   Any medical history
Accidents/incidents   Progress reports
Special dietary needs   Additional needs/support
Emergency contact number   Learning plans
GP details   Parents' mobile numbers
Any concerns about the child   Suspicion of abuse etc.

As you can see, this information is very important for the health and safety of the children. It needs to be written down and kept somewhere safe – not in someone's head!

Activity 8   Explanation

Points to make:

- As with reading, when we write in English we write from left to right, and from top to bottom.
- However, with writing there are a few more things to be aware of.
- Writing is more than just recording speech on paper – THERE ARE RULES TO BE FOLLOWED.
- Think about how we put expression into the words we say in order to communicate how we are feeling.

Activity 9   Discussion/idea storm – When we speak, how do we express ourselves?

Suggestions might include the following:

- Tone of voice
- Facial expression
- Stop
- Start

- Pause
- Gesture
- Words are spoken in an order that makes sense to the listener.

Explain that we need to put this same expression and order into our writing so that it makes sense to the reader.

Activity 10   Discussion – How do we add expression to our writing?

Ask the group for ideas and make sure that the following areas are covered:

- Punctuation
- Grammar
- Planning our writing
- Spelling words correctly
- Structuring our sentences and text
- Use of bold, italics or colour to stress a point.

Point out to learners that they will be developing these skills as they go along. For now, the concentration has to be on the mechanics of writing.

Activity 11   Focus exercise

Give out copies of Handout 5, 'Writing in English' and go through it with the students, reinforcing the points you have already discussed. Once you have been through the handout, give each student a copy of Activity Sheet 2, 'Different ways of writing' and ask them to complete the exercise.

Activity 12   Reflection

End the session by asking for feedback from the students on how they feel the work has gone.

HANDOUT 4

Reading in English

When we read the English language it is done in a particular way.

We read from the left of the page to the right of the page:

$$\longrightarrow$$

This way please

We read from the top of the page to the bottom of the page:

This

way

please

Whichever way the text is written, we read it in this way.

Different sorts of texts

These three texts are all written for different purposes. What do you think they are? (Write your answers alongside)

1. Tea
   Coffee
   Milk
   Sugar
   Bread

   ....

2. how r u?
   is yor cold btter?

   ....

3. Dear Tom,
   We are having a great
   holiday. The sun is shining
   and we are going to the
   beach later.
   See you next week,
             Sid and Doreen

   ....

HANDOUT 5

Writing in English

When we write the English language it is done in a particular way.

We write from the left of the page to the right of the page:

→

This way please

We write from the top of the page to the bottom of the page:

This

way

please

Whichever sort of text is being written, we write it in this way.

Different ways of writing

Writing can be structured in many different ways – it depends on what and why we are writing.

Take a look at the lists below.

Try to match the reason for writing (on the left) with the format (on the right). One has been done for you.

Shopping	Note in a diary
Asking people to your party	List
A letter to a friend	Form
Telling someone where and what time to meet you	Invitation
Applying for a job	A page or more of writing
An appointment time	Text message

SESSION 2

Outline

The main focus of this session is the alphabet. Remember the alphabet may seem basic and natural to us, but for a lot of people it is more complicated and will embarrass them. You will need to approach this sensitively if you are to generate enthusiasm in your students. Included in this session is an activity where learners are asked to make an alphabet poster for children. As well as being an enjoyable and creative activity, it takes the emphasis away from the learner, reinforcing learning through doing something fun for children.

For this session you will need:

- Flipchart showing the alphabet – make this as colourful as possible, with letters written in both upper and lower case.
- Cards with a mixture of upper case and lower case letters written on them.

Activities

Activity 1 **Introduction**

Remind learners that in the previous session you looked at reading and writing in a very broad way. The main points you considered were:

- Why we need to read and write.
- What reading and writing are.
- Basics of how to read and write.
- Rules and techniques and why we have them.

What you will be doing during Entry Level One is taking them through the skills, knowledge and understanding that they need in order to do it. Explain that in the forthcoming sessions you will be working on:

- Letters of the alphabet and how to form them
- Letter symbols and their sounds (sound/symbol association)
- Letter blends and how they sound
- Vowels and consonants
- Building words
- Building simple sentences
- Spelling
- Working out words for reading (decoding)
- Clues in text
- Basic punctuation for reading and writing
- Planning writing
- Different text types and their purpose
- Building an increasing list of words, signs and symbols you know on sight.

AND HAVING FUN WHILE DOING IT!!

Activity 2 Explanation

Make a start with the alphabet. This is the most important basis of literacy. If learners do not know the alphabet it can hinder them in so many ways.

Points to make:

- Students need to know the letters of the alphabet in order to use a dictionary.
- They need to be able to recognise letter names and sounds when reading, writing, forming and spelling words.
- Childcare students at placement will be working with children who are learning or even know the alphabet already. If they know it too it will enable them to work with and help the children more effectively and will help to boost their own self-confidence.

Activity 3 Group discussion – What is the alphabet?

Get a discussion underway with the following points:

- The alphabet has 26 letters set in a particular sequence.
- Each letter has a name.

Activity 4 Focus exercise

Ask learners to write down as much of the alphabet as they can. Once everyone has finished, display the alphabet flipchart and ask students to check their work, making any necessary corrections.

Go through the alphabet flipchart and explain about upper and lower case letters – which are which, etc. Tell the students that they will be going through uses of upper and lower case letters later on. For now, it is enough that they can identify them and write letters in upper and lower case.

Recite the alphabet aloud then ask students to go through it with you (how you do this depends very much on the learner group you have). As you go through reinforce the use of upper and lower case letters.

Give out copies of Handout 6, 'The alphabet' and go through it with the students, reinforcing what you have already explained.

Activity 5 Small group work – How much have we learned so far?

This activity begins by supporting students as they learn the letters of the alphabet in the correct sequence. It then gives them the opportunity to write the letters in upper and lower case.

How you put learners into groups will again depend on the learners you have. At this stage it is better for them to work alongside people with whom they feel comfortable. Some groups will need more support than others. Once these groups have been arranged, check that all students have a copy of Handout 6, 'The alphabet'.

Try working on the alphabet in small chunks, say five letters at a time. The best way to learn it is by reciting while looking at the letters, reciting while covering the letters, writing them down (upper and lower case), checking them (using Handout 6), then correcting them. Encourage students to try again and again until they pick it up!

What you give them to do now depends on what you think the learners can cope with. Ask for their opinions – they will feel more involved with their learning if you give them choices. Options might include the following:

• Ask students in their groups to write as much of the alphabet as they can remember on a flipchart. Display flipcharts and give a prize to the group with the most correct letters written in the right order. Keep the activity light and humorous.

• Ask students to write their names on a clean sheet of paper. Dictate the alphabet to them. Take the sheets in for marking to be given back next week.

• Dictate letters but not in alphabetical order. Either dictate them as 'write the letter a in upper case, write the letter d in lower case' or dictate letters and ask learners to write them in both upper and lower case.

Activity 6 Reflection

End the session by asking students to attempt the 'Alphabet activity' on Activity Sheet 3. Collect these in and spend some time after the session checking through their work in order to gauge levels of understanding.

The alphabet

Aa

    Bb

Cc

    Dd

Ee

    Ff

Gg

    Hh

Ii

    Jj

Kk

    Ll

Mm

    Nn

Oo

    Pp

Qq

    Rr

Ss

    Tt

Uu

    Vv

Ww

    Xx

Yy

    Zz

- The alphabet has 26 letters in a sequence
- Each letter has a name
- Each letter can be written in UPPER and lower case
- Five of the letters are <u>vowels</u>
- The other 21 are consonants
- The letter 'y' can sometimes be used as a vowel – but more about that later

20

Alphabet activity

Match the upper case letters to their lower case partners. One has been done for you in each column.

A	l	N	y
B	m	O	p
C	i	P	z
D	k	Q	w
E	g	R	u
F	a	S	v
G	j	T	t
H	d	U	s
I	e	V	q
J	b	W	o
K	f	X	n
L	c	Y	r
M	h	Z	x

© June Green (2003) *Basic Skills for Childcare – Literacy*. Published by David Fulton Publishers Ltd.

SESSION 3

Outline

In this session, learners are asked to make posters for children. This activity will reinforce what the learners have done so far and is relevant to their course and what they may be doing at placement. Quite a lot of the session will be taken up with poster-making, but it is well worth it. The exercise is designed to check learning and is an excellent excuse for the students to have a bit of fun.

Activities

Activity 1 Introduction

Start by distributing copies of Handout 7, 'Alphabet poster' to the students – one copy per person. The handout needs to be enlarged on a photocopier to the required size, depending on how big you intend the posters to be.

Give the following instructions to learners:

- Use the pictures in Handout 7 to make an attractive alphabet poster for children.
- Write the letters of the alphabet – in both upper and lower case – on a large sheet of plain paper.
- Carefully cut out the pictures from Handout 7 and put each one beside or underneath the appropriate letter.
- Write the word for the picture, with the initial letter highlighted, underneath the picture.

Two examples are shown in Figure 2.1. You might like to draw these on the flipchart to illustrate what you mean.

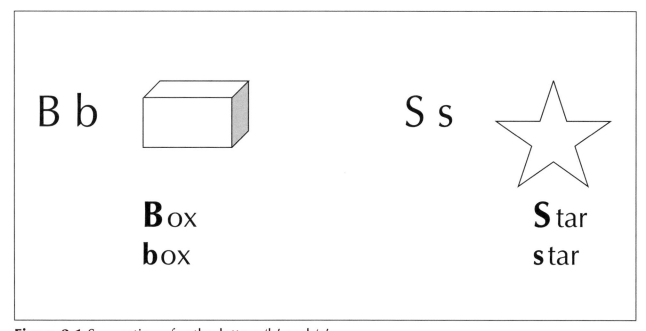

Figure 2.1 Suggestions for the letters 'b' and 's'

When this activity is finished talk to the learners about the skills they have been using – sequencing, spelling, use of upper and lower case letters. These are all skills needed for reading and writing, and didn't they have fun doing it?

Activity 2   Discussion/idea storm

Recap with the students: so far you have looked at the alphabet and seen that letters can be written in UPPER CASE (CAPITALS) and lower case (small) letters.

Most of what we read and write will be done in lower case letters. However, upper case letters are used in a variety of ways.

Ask the students to think of some instances when they have seen capital letters being used. List their suggestions on a flipchart. Below is an example of how this list might look:

- Beginning of a sentence
- People's names
- Names of places, e.g. towns, streets, etc.
- Days of the week
- Months of the year
- Special days, e.g. Christmas Day
- People's titles
- When talking about God
- Referring to yourself as 'I'
- Abbreviations
- Titles of books, films, TV programmes, etc.

Once the idea storming session is over, split the group into pairs or small groups. Give each pair/group a blank sheet of flipchart. Make sure they can see the original list and then ask them to come up with an example of each suggestion. You might like to give them some examples before they begin:

- Today we will . . .
- Christina, James
- Birmingham
- Monday
- September
- Christmas Day
- Ms, Mr
- God
- 'I am going to . . .'
- UK, USA
- Neighbours, Child Development

Finally, pool all the ideas in a group feedback exercise.

Activity 3 **Focus exercise**

When you think the students are happy with this, ask them to have a look at the activity on Activity Sheet 4. Focus on one text at a time. Read it out loud to the group and ask them to follow the words while you speak. Stop as you reach each number and ask the students to write down why the capital letter is being used.

As an extension exercise, there are some more short passages on Activity Sheet 5. Students could do these either during the session, or at home in their own time.

Alphabet poster

Cut these pictures out and use them to make an alphabet poster.

ACTIVITY SHEET 4

Below are some short texts. Can you work out what the capital letters are being used for? (Write your answers below)

TEXT A

Big Brother's Sophie Pritchard is set to emerge as one of the show's big winners after landing a sensational modelling offer.

The 25-year-old brunette is likely to pocket in the region of £70,000 as a new face of Head and Shoulders.

The recruitment consultant from Marlow, Bucks, will follow in the steps of Friends star Courtney Cox, 38, when she appears in the brand's advert.

1. _____   5. _____

2. _____   6. _____

3. _____   7. _____

4. _____   8. _____

TEXT B

| NCT (National Childbirth Trust) | Helps to give support and advice to parents to be and parents. There are 400 branches in the UK. | Alexandra House Oldham Road Acton London W3 6NH |

1. _____   3. _____

2. _____   4. _____

TEXT C

Voluntary organisations also provide learning and leisure activities for children – for example, Beavers, Brownies, Rainbows etc.

1. _____   2. _____

ACTIVITY SHEET 5

Below are some more short texts. Can you work out what the capital letters are being used for? (Write your answers below)

TEXT A

Early Years Directorate/OfSTED

As part of the National Childcare Strategy, the government wants all childminders, nursery schools and pre-schools to be inspected. The organisation for checking that childcare is of a good standard is the Office for Standards in Education (OfSTED).

1. _____   4. _____
2. _____   5. _____
3. _____

TEXT B

Albert Bandura (born 1925) was the first person to put forward the Social Learning theory. Bandura suggested that young children learn their behaviour from watching adults and others around them and copying what they see.

1. _____   3. _____
2. _____

TEXT C

Children start their compulsory education in the September nearest after their fourth birthday. For example:

Steve is four in May 2002, therefore he will start school in September 2002. Trish is four in November 2002, therefore she will start school in September 2003.

1. _____   4. _____
2. _____   5. _____
3. _____   6. _____

© June Green (2003) *Basic Skills for Childcare – Literacy*. Published by David Fulton Publishers Ltd.

SESSION 4

Outline

Previously you will have dictated the alphabet to your students as a way of familiarising them with the letter names. Now they know the names of the letters, the next stage is to make them familiar with the sounds.

For this session you will need:

• Blank sheets of flipchart and coloured pens.
• Cuttings from newspapers and magazines. These should be short, straightforward articles.

Activities

Activity 1   Introduction

Write the alphabet on the whiteboard or flipchart. Doing this in upper and lower case is an excellent way to reinforce previous learning. As you write, ask the students to call out the name of each letter.

Activity 2   Explanation

Tell the group that in addition to having a name, each letter has a sound. Ask the students if they know any. Go through the letters a few (five or six) at a time, giving each its sound and asking students to repeat them after you. After each set, pick different letters at random and ask students to give the sound. When you are happy that students have grasped letter sounds move on to the next activity.

Activity 3   Idea storm

Ask students if they can think of any funny ways to help them remember each letter's sound. Try starting them off with a couple of examples, e.g. 'dopey d', 'frantic f', 'queasy qu'. Ask them to work in small groups and to see if they can come up with some of their own. Tell them the sillier and more colourful they are the better!

You might want to give a few letters to each group or let them work randomly – you know their capability levels best. Give them a blank sheet of flipchart and lots of coloured pens so that they can write/illustrate their ideas. Display them around the room.

When you have something for each letter, get the pieces of work laminated and make a display of them in the classroom. Seeing these every day will not only help the students to remember them, it will also give them an enormous sense of pride in what they have done – this is extremely important in the early stages.

Activity 4 Focus exercise

Give each student five or six consonant sounds and a cutting from a newspaper or magazine. Ask them to find as many three- and four-letter words, containing the sounds you have given them, as they can.

Activity 5 Focus exercise

Put students into pairs and together go through Handout 8, 'They sound like this'. You might want to go through the first couple with them. This will give students a quick look at vowel sounds, which will be covered next session.

Activity 6 Reflection

End the session with a quick recap activity. Randomly call out consonant sounds and ask the students to write down the letter associated with the sound. Check their answers at the end of the exercise.

HANDOUT 8

They sound like this

Can you remember the five vowels?

a   e   i   o   u

Every word you use has at least one vowel in it.
Popular aren't they!

Have a look at these two words. They each have an 'o' in
them, but they sound different:

n<u>o</u>t   n<u>o</u>te

That's because the 'o' in n<u>o</u>t is using its *sound* and the 'o' in
n<u>o</u>te is using its *name*. These are known as *vowel sounds*.

The 'o' in n<u>o</u>t is using its *short vowel sound*.
The 'o' in n<u>o</u>te is using its *long vowel sound*.

ACTIVITY

Which are the long vowel sounds and which are the short
vowel sounds in each of these pairs:

b<u>e</u>t	h<u>e</u>
g<u>a</u>p	<u>a</u>pe
w<u>i</u>pe	s<u>i</u>p
h<u>o</u>t	ph<u>o</u>ne
s<u>u</u>e	h<u>u</u>t

SESSION 5

Outline

Having taken the students through consonant sounds you now need to go through vowel sounds. At this stage, keep it simple and go through short vowel sounds only.

Activities

Activity 1 **Introduction**

Remind students about the 'They sound like this' sheet you gave them in the previous session (Handout 8). Point out that although vowels have two sounds – a long sound and a short sound – you will only be working on short vowel sounds at this stage.

- Talk about the five vowels, giving each of them their sound.
- Give each student a copy of Activity Sheet 6, 'Short vowel sounds' and ask them to complete the exercise.
- As an extension to Activity Sheet 6 ask the students what the 'Escape to victory' article is about and where they think it came from, e.g. a newspaper, magazine, TV guide. What is it trying to tell us?

Sld/E1.1

Ww/E1.3

Activity 2 **Focus exercise**

Write each of the five vowels on a flipchart. Ask students to come up with as many vowel/consonant/vowel words as they can, for example *tap, pen, hip, got, nut*. The vowel must be using its short sound. Give them about ten to fifteen minutes to come up with them.

When time is up ask the students to give you their suggestions and write them on the appropriate flipchart. Go through their list and see how many of them rhyme.

Activity 3 **Focus exercise**

This is a fun activity. Ask students to come up with as many three-letter, rhyming nonsense words as they can, for example *jop, lup, fap, tep, bip*. This activity will give the students practice in using letters to compose words. The rhyming and the nonsense elements make the exercise easier for them. They will be saying, seeing and repeating the letters and sounds while building their 'nonsense' words.

When they have done this, give the students the choice of either: (a) reading out their words which you then write on the board; or (b) writing them on flipcharts using different coloured pens for each vowel sound. The flipchart option is usually more fun!

Activity 4 **Focus exercise**

Now ask the students to pick one of their 'nonsense' words and come up with a meaning for it. Give them Handout 9, 'Mips' as an example. These pieces of work can be made into a display headed 'What a load of nonsense'.

Activity 5 Reflection

Explain to students that through these activities they have been:

- Learning about letter sounds
- Spelling
- Rhyming
- Composing
- Reading
- HAVING FUN WHILE DOING IT!

End the session with a recap quiz on consonant and short vowel sounds.

Short vowel sounds

Highlight the words using their short vowels sound in the article below.

Escape to victory

Big Brother, Channel 4, all week.

By managing to avoid eviction and stay in the Big Brother house for the whole ten weeks, the show's four remaining contestants have missed an awful lot of real life. From the Golden Jubilee celebrations, to the highs and lows of the World Cup and Greg and Tim at Wimbledon, a great deal's been happening while they've been away. But this week it's time for them to leave the house and rejoin the rest of us, as the show reaches its dramatic climax and moment of truth on Friday. As always Davina McCall is your host, as the public choose who will be crowned winner of Big Brother 3 . . .

From:

What's on THIS WEEK

Saturday 20th July to Friday 26th July 2002

Mips

Mips are a very friendly people from the planet MIPE.

MIPS are a gorgeous violet colour with one eye at the front of their head and one at the back – a distinct disadvantage for their children as the adults can see everything that goes on.

Having an eye at the back of their head, Mips are also able to walk backwards, which comes in very useful if they ever have to go back for something. They just start running backwards. They are very friendly people, love entertaining and their favourite place to take visitors is the PIME DISCO. Everyone really lets their hair down (a figure of speech, as MIPS have no hair). But they really do know how to have a good time.

Food on the planet is delicious. Their national dish is called PESTA PONNE, a mixture of short fat tube-like things and very long thin string-like things covered in a brown sauce (resembling chocolate) and topped with moon flowers. It actually tastes very nice.

A visit to the people of MIPE promises to be a good one!

SESSION 6

Outline

You have taken students through the consonant and short vowel sounds.

Point out that there are many, many more sounds in the English language than the sounds of the alphabet. This is what makes English so difficult for a lot of people to learn. These sounds are called 'phonemes' – the smallest meaningful sound made in a word. They can be made up of one or more letters.

> For this session you will need:
>
> • A selection of children's storybooks.

Activities

Activity 1 Introduction

Begin the session by writing the words *name*, *address*, *day* and *week* on the board/flipchart. See if the students can break these words down into their phonemes. Explain to them that they now need to work on phonemes and that they will start with:

• Consonant sounds that can be spelt in different ways, e.g. ph = 'f'
• Silent letters
• Hard and soft letters and their sounds.

The focus of this session can get a bit complicated but it is worth spending time on it. What you do now will form the basis of your students' future reading and writing. It should also make life easier for you when it comes to marking their written work!

Now is a good time to tell students to start using the spelling and dictionary pages in their Workbooks.

Activity 2 Reflection

Remind students about consonants and short vowel sounds learnt so far. A short recap at this stage will jog a few memories and prepare them for the rest of the session.

Activity 3 Explanation

• Explain to your students that many of the sounds they have learnt can be spelt in different ways.
• Have a look at Figure 2.2. Write the words that are in bold on the board and keep the layout the same as it is in the diagram.
• Ask students what sounds the underlined letters make and then take them through how they are spelt.
• Point out that although some of them are spelt the same way they do not sound the same.
• Explain that there are some consonant sounds that can be spelt in several ways.
• Give out copies of Handout 10, 'Crafty consonants' and go through it with the students.

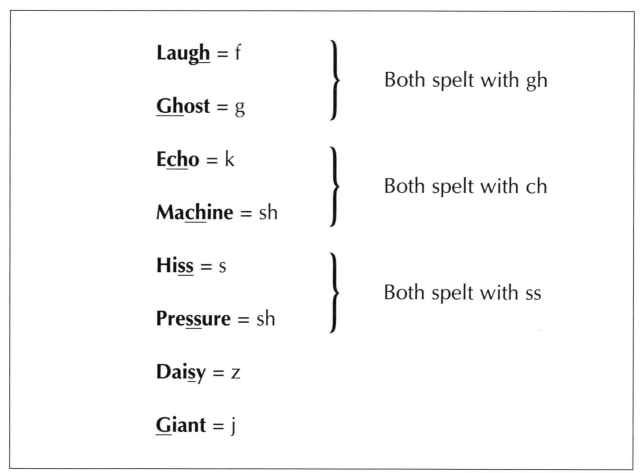

Figure 2.2 Consonant sounds that can be spelt in different ways

Activity 4 **Focus exercise**

When you are sure the students have grasped the points covered in Activity 3, ask them to try and make up some silly rhymes for children, using some of the sounds from Handout 10. Here's an example: *The queen gave the giraffe a kiss. The giraffe turned into the king and the nation rejoiced.*

Activity 5 **Explanation**

The next thing you need to look at is silent letters.

- Explain to students that in English there are lots of words that contain silent letters. Although the letters are silent they always have to be included when the word is written down so that it can be spelt correctly and will therefore make sense.
- Write the following words on the board without saying them: *wren, autumn, listen, lamb.* Ask students if they can tell you the silent letter in each of them:

wren = w
autumn = n
listen = t
lamb = b

- Give out copies of Handout 11, 'Sh – silent letters' and go through it with the students.
- When you have done that, have a bit of fun saying words with the silent letters pronounced in an exaggerated way. Tell students it might help them to use this as a memory trick when spelling these words.
- Give out children's storybooks and ask the students to find words with silent letters in them.
- Take feedback at the end of the session.

Crafty consonants

F

The sound 'f' as in football can be spelt like this:

- 'f' as in <u>f</u>ood
- 'ff' as in gira<u>ff</u>e
- 'gh' as in lau<u>gh</u>
- 'ph' as in <u>ph</u>easant

G

The sound of 'g' as in girl can be spelt like this:

- 'g' as in <u>g</u>oat
- 'gg' as in e<u>gg</u>
- 'gh' as in <u>gh</u>ost
- 'gu' as in <u>gu</u>itar

J

The sound of 'j' as in jump can be spelt like this:

- 'dg' as in fu<u>dg</u>e
- 'g' as in <u>g</u>iant
- 'j' as in <u>j</u>oke

S

The sound of 's' as in social can be spelt like this:

- 'ce' as in mi<u>ce</u>
- 's' as in <u>s</u>nake
- 'sc' as in <u>sc</u>ent
- 'ss' as in hi<u>ss</u>

K

The sound of 'k' as in king can be spelt like this:

- 'c' as in cat
- 'cc' as in accordion
- 'ch' as in echo
- 'ck' as in duck
- 'k' as in kind
- 'qu' as in quiche
- 'que' as in cheque

SH

The sound of 'sh' as in share can be spelt like this:

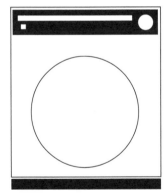

- 'ch' as in machine
- 'ci' as in special
- 's' as in sugar
- 'sh' as in shampoo
- 'si' as in pension
- 'ssi' as in mission
- 'ss' as in pressure
- 'ti' as in nation

Z

The sound of 'z' as in zebra can be spelt like this:

- 's' as in daisy
- 'z' as in lazy

Rw/E1.2
Ww/E1.3

HANDOUT 11

Sh – silent letters

B

'b' is silent after 'm' as in *lamb* or *thumb*

G

'g' is silent before noisy 'n' as in *sign* or *gnat*

GH

'gh' is silent when it comes in at the end as in *dough* or *through*

or

when it comes before talkative 't' as in *bright* or *brought*

H

'h' is silent at the beginning as in *honest* or *hour*

or

when 'r' is first as in *rhyme* or *rhythm*

K

'k' is always silent when it comes before 'n' as in *knee* and *knife*

L

'l' is silent in *talk* and *half*

N

'n' is silent when 'm' comes first as in *autumn* or *hymn*

P

'p' is silent when 's', 'n' or 't' are there before it as in *psalm* or *pneumonia*

S

's' is silent in *island* and *aisle*

T

't' is silent when 's' comes first as in *listen* and *castle*
and
'ch' makes it hard to hear 't' as in *match* and *hutch*

W

'w' is silent before 'r' as in *write* and *wrist*
and
sometimes before 'h' as in *who* and *whole*

SESSION 7

Outline

In this session the focus will be on consonant clusters. Some students might start to get a bit confused and 'worried' at this point. They will need extra support and time. It's worth having some word-searches or other word games for others to be doing if you find that some students need extra attention from you.

For this session you will need:

- Some nonsense verse books or poetry books – these can be children or adult versions, depending on which are more fun!

- A few short stories or some articles from a newspaper.

Activities

Activity 1 Introduction

So far most of the emphasis has been on letters and their sounds. It is now time to move on to what we call 'consonant clusters'. Explain that consonant clusters are small clusters of letters that when put together make a sound e.g. *sp, spl, ld, sk*.

Write these on the board and ask students if they can think of any words using these clusters. Suggestions might include the following:

- spot
- splash
- fold
- mask.

Point out that some of these clusters will be found at the beginning of words and are known as 'initial consonant clusters'; others will be found at the end of words and are known as 'final consonant clusters'.

Activity 2 Explanation

Give out copies of Handout 12, 'Consonant clusters' and go through it with the students. Work on a few at a time, stopping to ask learners whether they can think of any words that contain these clusters.

Extend this activity by handing out Activity Sheet 7, 'Initial consonant clusters' and Activity Sheet 8, 'Final consonant clusters' and asking the students to come up with examples for each cluster. You might choose to do a few in each session if concerned that the exercise might become too stale. You know how much the group can cope with before boredom sets in, so it's really up to you to decide how many to tackle at any one time.

Activity Sheet 9, 'Missing consonant clusters' has been provided as a further extension activity, which learners can take away and try in their own time.

`Activity 3` Focus exercise

Divide the students into twos and give each pair a selection of verse books and newspaper articles. Ask them to see if they can find any consonant clusters and to tell you whether these are initial or final clusters.

`Activity 4` Group discussion

As a bit of fun ask each student to choose their favourite nonsense verse. Take turns reading them out and talk about which elements in the poems appeal to the students.

`Activity 5` Focus exercise

Rt/EL1
Rs/EL1
Rw/EL1

End with a game called 'What's my cluster?'. This is a great way to reinforce what has already been learnt during the session.

Put students into teams. From the consonants clusters list on Handout 12, pick a few clusters and say them out loud to the students. Ask them to write down the cluster they think you are sounding out. The 'winner' is the team who gets the most right. Reward the winning team in some way – an extra five minutes at break-time is a real favourite!

HANDOUT 12

Consonant clusters

Consonant clusters are small groups of consonants that make sounds at the beginning and ends of words.

For example:

sl as in **sl**eep
cr as in **cr**eam
scr as in **scr**eam

and

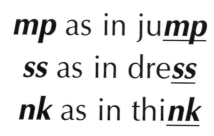

mp as in ju**mp**
ss as in dre**ss**
nk as in thi**nk**

Ww/E1.3

Initial consonant clusters

In the first column is a list of initial consonant clusters and an example of how they can be used. See if you can write your own examples in the second column.

'sk' as in skate	
'sp' as in spoon	
'st' as in stamp	
'sc' as in scale	
'sm' as in smile	
'sn' as in snow	
'sl' as in sleep	
'sw' as in swim	
'tw' as in twist	
'dw' as in dwarf	
'cr' as in crown	
'gr' as in grape	
'fr' as in frown	
'thr' as in three	
'spr' as in spray	
'bl' as in blue	
'cl' as in clown	
'gl' as in glass	
'fl' as in flag	
'pr' as in prize	
'br' as in bread	
'tr' as in tree	
'dr' as in drink	
'pl' as in play	
'squ' as in square	
'spl' as in splash	
'shr' as in shrub	
'str' as in street	
'scr' as in screw	

46

Final consonant clusters

ACTIVITY SHEET 8

In the first column is a list of final consonant clusters and an example of the use of them. See if you can write your own examples in the second column.

'ld' as in cold	
'nd' as in hand	
'lk' as in milk	
'nk' as in think	
'sk' as in ask	
'lp' as in help	
'mp' as in bump	
'sp' as in wasp	
'ct' as in fact	
'ft' as in gift	
'lt' as in kilt	
'nt' as in want	
'pt' as in slept	
'st' as in list	
'xt' as in next	
'lf' as in half	
'nch' as in bunch	
'lth' as in wealth	
'ck' as in sick	
'll' as in fall	
'ss' as in mess	
'ng' as in ring	

© June Green (2003) *Basic Skills for Childcare – Literacy*. Published by David Fulton Publishers Ltd.

Missing consonant clusters

Here are some words you will come across during your course. Some have the initial consonant clusters missing, some have the final consonant clusters missing. Try putting them in.

Sa

ay

aining

ills

Chi

othes

elling

Assignme

udents

Hea

Conce

Te

Session 8

Outline

Start this session by going through what the students have been working on and talking about what they have learnt so far. They are likely to be surprised (and pleased) at what they have achieved. It has taken them a great deal of hard work to get this far and a massive amount of praise is due to them. The early levels of literacy are always that bit tougher than the later levels and require a lot of staying power. So well done to them and to you!

For Part 1 of this session you will need:

• Some blank postcards.

For Part 2 you will need:

• A set of cards with one of the following words written on each: *on, high, low, only, want, first, have, them, open, right, front, was.*
• Some copies of TV guides.

Activities

Activity 1 **Introduction**

• Tell the students that having spent quite a lot of time on letters, they are now going to use these skills to work on words. Explain that a lot of words they will come across during this session will already be familiar to them because they see and use them often. At this level you will be working on:

  – Personal keywords
  – Familiar words
  – Social sight vocabulary
  – Sight vocabulary of words and signs

• Tell the students that you need some information to give to their placement. As you do so, write these words on the board:

  Name:
  Address:
  Telephone number:

• Ask them to copy what you've written onto a sheet of paper and to fill in the details for you. Tell them to ask for help if they need it and that you will check their work once they've finished. This will give you a chance to assess whether they can read and write key personal words.

• Explain to students that to give this information in writing they have to be able to read and spell some personal keywords, e.g. name, address and telephone number. Can students think of any other key personal words they might need to know? (For example, date of birth, where they were born, age, medical conditions, children's names and date of birth, names and addresses of friends and family, etc.)

- As an extension activity, ask students to complete as much as possible of 'Personal words' page in their Workbooks. Remind them to bring this work to the next session so that you can review what they have done.

Activity 2 Explanation

Points to make:

- Explain that as well as personal key words there are 'high-frequency' words that they need to know.
- High-frequency words are words that you see and use over and over again. You see them in text, you say them, you write them down. Ask the students whether they can think of any examples.
- Give out copies of Handout 13, 'Well-used words' and go through it with the students. Emphasise that no-one expects anyone to know/learn all of these at once! It is a gradual process.
- While going through this handout, stress that:

  - these are considered to be important words in learning to read (called the Dolch list)
  - each word has its own meaning
  - they are frequently used words
  - some are easier to recognise than others (discuss why this might be).

- Agree with students how frequently you will check their progress on this, and make sure you build in time for it – perhaps at the beginning or end of sessions.

Activity 3 Discussion/idea storm

Another group of words we need to look at are called 'social sight vocabulary'.

These are words that you know without having to decode them. You know them on sight because you see them, write them and say them all the time, e.g. *on/off*.

Together, see how many words you can think of that might be in this group. Where might you see them?

Give out copies of Handout 14, 'Social sight vocabulary' and discuss the words with the students. Focus in on the days of the week, then divide the students into twos and give each pair a cutting from a TV guide. Ask them to circle all the times the days of the week are mentioned. The object of this activity is to point out how often these words are used in one place.

Activity 4 Focus exercise

Spend the rest of the session helping students to compose some simple messages – lists, reminders, notes to friends, notes to a child's school, and so on – using words from the lists you have worked on. Encourage students to use some words they are familiar with and some they are not. (Whenever they get stuck on a word, encourage them to use the 'look, say, cover, write, check' method, or to trace the letters of the word with their fingers.)

Activity 5 **Reflection**

End the session with a fun group activity which will reinforce previous learning and emphasise the 'real-life' element of the activities.

Put students into groups and ask them to compose a short message, on a sheet of flipchart, to a politician. They can say anything they like – as long as they use some of the words they have worked on today.

HANDOUT 13

Well-used words

This is a list of high-frequency words. These are words that occur a lot in day-to-day life. These are words that will slow down the reading progress if they are not known.

A	Other	Her	Said
I	Night	Into	We
It	Some	Little	About
The	Then	Make	Been
All	Two	Much	By
Be	Well	No	Can
For	What	Off	Did
His	Which	Or	First
On	And	Out	Go
So	In	See	Here
With	Of	Their	Just
An	To	There	Look
Before	As	Up	More
Call	But	Went	Must
Come	Had	When	New
Do	Him	Will	Old
From	One	Your	Our
Has	They	He	Over
If	You	Is	She
Like	Back	That	Them
Made	Big	Was	This
Me	Come	At	Want
My	Could	Are	Why
Now	Down	Have	How
Only	Get	Not	Who

Go through this list. How many words do you know without having to work them out, how many can you work out easily and how many are really difficult for you?

Your tutor will discuss this with you and make a plan for you to begin learning the rest by sight. Don't worry – you'll only have to learn a few at a time!

HANDOUT 14

Social sight vocabulary

Social sight vocabulary are words that you know without decoding them. You know them on sight because you see them, write them and say them a lot, e.g. 'on/off'.

on	off	salt	sugar	tea

coffee   front   back   left

right   shampoo   poison

Monday   Tuesday   Wednesday   Thursday

Friday   Saturday   Sunday

January   February   March

April   May   June

July   August   September

October   November   December

year   parcels   top   bottom

careful   fragile   urgent

'open here'   'open other side'

'this way up'   'handle with care'

SESSION 9

Outline

So far the concentration has been on words and how to spell them, how they sound, how to write them and decode them. The object of this session is to use these word skills to WRITE.

Activities

Activity 1 | Introduction

• Tell the students that you are now going to look at SENTENCES.
• Ask the question 'What is a sentence?' and idea storm a list of suggestions, discussing each one in turn.
• Give out copies of Handout 15, 'Sentences' and go through it with the students. Point out that at this level you will be working on simple sentences.
• Next ask each student to write two sentences about children. These can be based on anything they like. Check that capital letters and full stops have been used correctly, and that words are in the right order so as to make sense.
• Once they have finished writing their sentences, hold a discussion to see if the students can think of different types of sentences.
• To round off this stage of the session, give out copies of Handout 16, 'Sentence types and their uses' and go through it with the students.

Activity 2 | Explanation

Points to make:

• We know what a sentence is, we know we can use them to write down what we want to say. But before we start it is important to understand that writing is not just a matter of putting down on paper what we want to say. There are rules!
• Think about it! When we speak to communicate, we put expression into what we are saying by varying our tone of voice, stopping, starting, pausing and using different facial expressions and gestures. We put our words into an order that makes sense.
• So how do we put expression into our writing? We do it by using writing 'rules' that enable us to write something that makes sense, so that the reader can understand what we are saying. These rules include:

 – Punctuation
 – Grammar
 – Planning writing
 – Spelling
 – Structuring writing.

We will be working on some of these rules throughout this level.

Activity 3   **Focus exercise**

Explain to students that you are going to start working on some of the rules for writing. Knowing these rules not only helps us with our writing, it can also help to improve our reading. For example, if you read a sentence that ends in a question mark, you know it is asking a question. Remind students that they will be working on simple sentences only.

Give out copies of Handout 17, 'Simple sentence rules' and go through it with the students. When you are sure that learners are familiar with the rules, ask them to do the activity on the handout.

Discuss the answers to the activity, pointing out the following:

• The subject of each sentence is the children.
• Sentence 1 tells you something about the children – is a *statement*.
• Sentence 2 gives an instruction to be carried out with the children – is a *command*.
• Sentence 3 asks something about the children – is a *question*.
• Sentence 4 tells us something about the children, with expression – is an *exclamation*.

Mention to the students that it doesn't matter where the subject comes in the sentence. If you look at the four sentences, the subject is at the beginning in three of the sentences and in the middle of the other one.

Activity 4   **Focus exercise**

Explain to the students the importance of remembering to use punctuation when writing. They already know what a sentence begins and ends with, but now they need to be introduced to some other forms of punctuation. Give students copies of Activity Sheet 10, 'Where's my punctuation?' to do individually or in pairs. Go through their answers once they have finished.

Activity 5   **Explanation**

Explain to learners that when we talk we start speaking to begin and stop to end. Students need to think of punctuation as the 'stops' and 'starts' of writing.

Give out copies of Handout 18, 'Playing happily'. Go through the handout with the students, pointing out that in the first piece of text it sounds as though the child was playing happily on the climbing frame ten minutes after he had fallen off and bumped his head! Explain that by adding some punctuation, the sentence makes more sense.

Ask students to write three simple sentences about something they have done at placement/college recently. Remind them to use writing rules and to check their spelling. Have a look at their work once they have finished.

Sentences

- Sentences are the basic building blocks of continuous text.
- They are used to record information and convey a message.
- Sentences are a way of representing language.
- A sentence is a group of words, set down in order, that makes complete sense on its own. It has two parts:

1. The subject – who or what the sentence is about
2. The predicate – information about the subject

For example:

The nursery-nurse (subject)   <u>was reading a story.</u>
<u>(predicate)</u>

Sentence types and their uses

Sentences have a number of different purposes:

STATEMENTS – sentences that state fact, e.g. *'Today is Tuesday.'*

QUESTIONS – sentences that ask for an answer, e.g. *' What lesson do we have first on Tuesday?'*

COMMANDS – sentences that give orders or commands, e.g. *'You must be back from your break at 10.30 a.m.'*

EXCLAMATIONS – sentences that express strong feelings or emotions, or indicate shouting, e.g. *'I really love you!'*

Simple sentence rules

(Remember that at this point we are working on simple sentences only.)

- Every sentence contains a verb, at least one subject and one predicate.
- Every sentence begins with a capital letter.
- Every sentence ends with a punctuation mark.
- In simple sentences we use short familiar words to be direct and interesting.
- Simple sentences have only one subject and one predicate.
- They are short, sharp and to the point, for example:

The student was changing the baby's nappy.

The children are changing for PE.

ACTIVITY

Below are four sentences. What is the subject of each sentence?

1. The children are going to the science museum tomorrow.
2. Do not allow the children into the kitchen.
3. Are the children ready to go out to play?
4. The children are very noisy today!

ACTIVITY SHEET 10

Where's my punctuation?

The sentences below are missing their punctuation. Some are commands, some are statements, some are questions and some are exclamations.

Try putting in the punctuation marks for each one.

- how many words can children say at the age of four years

- your assignment must be handed in on Tuesday

- the children loved playing in the snow

- i hate the cold weather

- the children worked hard today

- stop now

- at what age do babies start to crawl

- they are so excited

HANDOUT 18

Playing happily

Read the following two passages. Which one makes most sense?

1 | the little boy was playing happily on the climbing frame ten minutes after he fell off and bumped his head hard.

2 | The little boy was playing happily on the climbing frame. Ten minutes after, he fell off and bumped his head hard.

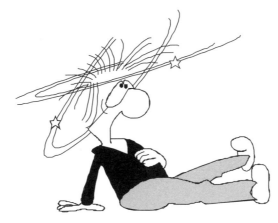

Speaking and Listening activities for Entry Level One

For this session you will need:

- Different sets of written instructions for putting on a baby's nappy and getting a baby's bath ready.
- A pre-prepared message from you to the students about a visit to the town/city library. This should contain simple details, e.g. where it is, time to meet and why you are going.

Activities

Activity 1

In pairs, students should take turns being the instructor and the listener. Each pair should have a set of both instructions. As instructors, they should read the instructions to their partner. As listeners, they should be able to show they are listening, ask for clarification on any points they do not understand and respond to their instructor by carrying out the instructions.

➤ After each student has had a turn at being the instructor and listener, hold a group discussion to find out how students thought the exercise went. Who felt they needed to listen carefully? Which students felt they only had to listen just for the gist? Why?

Activity 2

Explain to students that you are going to read out a simple message about a visit they are going on. Tell them that when you have finished reading the message, you want them to write out the main points for a student who is absent from college today.

➤ Check from their written message that all students have taken in the detail.

Activity 3

Students should prepare some requests for personal information, e.g. what is your address, when is your birthday, when were you born, where were you born, etc.

In pairs, students should take turns asking and responding to the questions.

Activity 4

SLd/
EW1.1
SLc/E1.1

Show a video, e.g. an episode (or part of it) of a popular soap drama. Ask students to see what they notice about body language, facial expression, any gestures used, etc. Discuss what these non-verbal signals could mean, e.g. that characters are amused, defensive, edgy, listening carefully, and so on.

➤ Ensure that each student takes part in this discussion.

Activity 5

SLc/E1.3

Idea storm situations where students might need to ask for specific information.

➤ This activity is best done in pairs.

Each student should pick a situation in which they would need to ask for help and/or information, e.g. to find out about a course, or to find their way to a place. They should think of specific questions that might need to be asked. Pairs should then take it in turns to role-play scenarios in which they are asking for help and/or information.

CHAPTER 3

Entry Level Two

Introduction

Having built up the basics in Entry Level One it is now time for your students to move on. Still working at a relatively basic level, in Entry Level Two they will be building on skills covered in Entry Level One, as well as developing a variety of new skills.

Students can expect to cover some aspects of the following at this level:

- Punctuation
- Proper nouns
- Spelling
- Grammar
- Recognising more complicated words
- Using spelling patterns
- Using phonic and graphic strategies to help spelling
- Using a dictionary
- Reading and understanding short, straightforward texts
- Reading to obtain information
- Listening to, and responding to, spoken language, e.g. instructions
- Speaking to communicate feelings and opinions
- Engaging in discussion with one or more people in a familiar situation.

It is clear from the above that students will be revisiting topics covered during Entry Level One. This means that there will be plenty of opportunities for students to practise the skills they have already learnt. Using a dictionary, for example, builds on the alphabet skills developed in the previous level.

SESSION 1

Outline

The object of this session is to recap what was covered in Entry Level One and to explain to students that in this level they will be building on the skills they have already gained as well as developing some new ones.

In Activities 1 and 2 students are encouraged to make connections between new and previously covered topics as a way of promoting understanding and to help them learn more effectively. Activities 3–9 introduce the subject of spelling.

Activities

Activity 1   Introduction

Using the list from the introduction to this chapter, go through the skills that students will be developing at Entry Level Two. Some learners might be worried about the amount of work they will be covering in this level. Reassure the group that many of these skills will be covered simultaneously and that the whole process will be taken a step at a time, at the student's own pace.

Activity 2   Group discussion

Discuss with students which topics link together or build on skills they learnt during Entry Level One. You might like to start them off with one of the following suggestions:

- Using a dictionary builds on alphabet skills.
- Using capitals for proper nouns (names) builds on using upper and lower case letters.
- Using phonic (sound) and graphic (symbol) strategies links with spelling, reading, writing and speaking (reading aloud).
- Speaking to communicate opinions and feelings links to engaging in discussion.

Point out that everything that is learnt is useful and necessary. Nothing is ever wasted.

Activity 3   Discussion/recap

Spelling is at the core of Entry Level Two, so now would be as good a time as any to ask students how they feel about it. This usually turns out to be quite an interesting exercise – people's feelings about their spelling ability are often strong and it is worth spending some time discussing problem areas so that certain taboos can be overcome. The object of the next few activities will be to encourage the students to get their feelings about spelling off their chest and to prove to them that with a little practice they can learn to spell.

As part of your introduction to the topic of spelling, do a recap exercise in which you start by explaining to students that they have explored the 26 letters of the alphabet and that you would now like them to give you examples of the following:

- How the letters are written.
- The sounds they make on their own and when put together with other letters.
- Which are vowels and which are consonants.

Remind students that these 26 letters and the sounds they make are what we use to build words.

Activity 4 Focus exercise

- Distribute copies of Handout 19, 'Spelling' around the room and go through it with the students.
- Next give out copies of Activity Sheet 11, 'How I feel about spelling' and ask students to write down – individually or in pairs – how they feel about spelling. This will give you an early indication of their concerns relating to what they have covered so far in this session.

Activity 5 Group discussion

Discuss students' responses and why they feel the way they do. Encourage everyone in the group to take part, as by doing so they will be reinforcing some of their Speaking and Listening skills. You might want to give them a couple of examples to get the ball rolling, e.g. 'I enjoy it' or 'It's difficult'.

Activity 6 Idea storm

By now the group will have made their views on spelling abundantly clear (I've yet to meet a group that hasn't!). Now that they have voiced their feelings, get them to start thinking about what spelling really is. A good way to approach this is by asking the following questions:

- What is spelling?
- Why do we find it so difficult?

Ask students to make suggestions and list these on the flipchart. From this list try and come up with a group definition of spelling, which everyone agrees on. Display the final definition somewhere in the classroom.

Activity 7 Explanation

Give out copies of Handout 20, 'Spelling is . . .' and go through each point with the students. Stress to the group that while spelling is only one part of writing, it is important for people working with young children to get it right.

Activity 8 Focus exercise

- Say the word 'orlop' to the group and ask them to write it down. Don't tell them how to spell it, even if they ask.
- Invite the students to call out some of the ways they have spelt it. Possible answers might include: 'aulop', 'aurlop', 'alop' and 'oarlop'. Write their suggestions on the board.
- Point out that all/nearly all their answers could be right. Look at the letter combinations they have used at the beginning of the words. All of the ones listed above could have been correct, and all of the endings were right.
- The aim of this activity is to prove to the students that they can all spell to some degree, and that they do this by sound/symbol combination.
- Incidentally, an 'orlop' is the lowest deck in a ship with more than three decks.

Activity 9 **Focus exercise**

End the session by asking students to do the 'What do I need to do to spell correctly?' activity in their Workbooks (p. 17). Before they begin, explain that the group will be working on some spelling strategies during the next two sessions, but the process of learning to spell well will take time and commitment.

Spelling

- To be written down, words need to be spelt out.

- Spelling is putting letters in the right order to make words.

- The same word is always spelt in the same way, whenever you read or write it.

- Words have meanings, so for our writing to make sense we need to:

  ➤ put the right word

  ➤ spelt correctly

  ➤ in the right place.

How I feel about spelling

Use the space below to draw or write down how you feel about spelling.

SPELLING

Spelling is...

✳ Something we do every day.

✳ Something we might need to help children with while we are at placement.

✳ Something we can all do to some level – yes we can!

✳ Something we need to do if we want people to understand what we write.

✳ Something we need to use to help us make sense of writing.

✳ Important, but it's ONLY ONE PART OF WRITING.

✳ Hard to do in English because English is a complicated language.

✳ Something we can all improve on –YES WE CAN!

✳ Setting out letters in the correct order to make words sound right. Words need to sound right for writing to make sense.

✳ 'Something that sounds easy, but I can't do it' – YES YOU CAN!

SESSION 2

Outline

In this session the students will begin to work on spelling. Reassure them that this is where they will make a START. You won't expect everyone to have good spelling skills by the end of this session. It takes time, patience and hard work from the learners themselves and from you as their tutor.

For this session you will need:

- An assortment of texts for paired work on vowel phonemes, e.g. newspaper articles, magazine interviews, children's storybooks, etc.

Activities

Activity 1 Introduction

Review the Workbook activity that students were given to do at the end of the previous session ('What do I need to do to spell correctly?'). Discuss the suggestions they have come up with. Explain that many if not all the things they have mentioned will be covered in the Basic Skills sessions within Entry Level Two.

Activity 2 Explanation

Tell the students that they are now going to look at more letter sounds. Point out that:

- Knowledge of sound–letter correspondence is important for both reading and writing.
- The group worked on some vowel sounds, consonant cluster sounds, etc. in Entry Level One, so this will be a good opportunity to do some revision!
- The object of this session will be to work on some more sounds. When the students have done this the group will look at some strategies to help spelling.
- For most people, spelling does not come naturally – it has to be learnt.

Activity 3 Focus exercise

Recap vowel sounds covered in the previous level:

- Give each student a copy of Activity Sheet 12, 'Playgroup' and ask them to complete the exercise.
- When everyone has finished discuss answers as a group. (These have been provided for you in Figure 3.1.) If the words 'playing', 'playgroup', 'activities' and 'leaving' are suggested, point out that while they do contain a long vowel sound the vowel does not make the sound on its own, e.g. in 'playing' the 'a' sound is made by the letters 'a' and 'y' together.
- Move on to Activity Sheet 13, 'The long and the short of it'. Some students may get through this activity quicker than others – if they do, ask them to put the words into alphabetical order.
- Discuss answers together once everyone has finished. (These have been provided for you in Figure 3.2.)

Tutor's answers to 'Playgroup' activity	Short vowel sound = ... Long vowel sound = ___

From the age of two years a child may go to a playgroup. Going to playgroup helps children to develop their social skills, get used to other carers and take part in a variety of activities. They have experience of a different type of routine, working and playing with other children and they get used to their parents leaving and coming back for them.

(NOTE: Some students might include 'playing', 'playgroup', 'activities' and 'leaving'. These are not correct as the vowel is not making the long sound on its own.)

Figure 3.1 Answers to exercise on Activity Sheet 12

SHORT VOWEL SOUNDS			LONG VOWEL SOUNDS		
songs	o		baby	a	
allergies	a		clothes	o	
imaginative	i	a	respect	e	
college	o		music	u	
respect	e		emotional	e	o
music	i		viruses	i	
cuts	u		time	i	
emotional	a				
viruses	u	e			
helper	e				
values	a				
cultures	u				

Figure 3.2 Answers to exercise on Activity Sheet 13

Activity 4 Explanation/idea storm

Explain that as well as vowels having their own long sound, they can make long sounds when combined with other letters. Remind the students about 'playing', 'playgroup', 'activities' and 'leaving' from 'Playgroup' activity (Activity Sheet 12). In other words some sounds can be made in a variety of ways – one reason why the English language is so complicated and difficult for so many to learn.

- Give out copies of Handout 21, 'Long vowel phonemes' and see if students can think of any words that use any of these phonemes.
- Put students into pairs/groups and ask them to come up with lists of words using the same long vowel pattern.
- Ask learners to read out their suggestions and list these on a flipchart. Discuss feedback.

Activity 5 Explanation/focus exercise

Another set of phonemes learners need to become familiar with are common vowel phonemes.

- Start by giving out copies of Handout 22, 'Common vowel phonemes' and go through it with the students.
- Arrange the students into pairs and give out the texts you collected before the start of the session – at least two to each student – and ask learners to read them to their partner. See if they can note down any words that use the vowel phonemes listed on Handout 22, and encourage them to use their knowledge of vowel phonemes to decode unknown words.
- Make a list of unfamiliar words to look up later.

Activity 6 Focus exercise

End the session with a team game. On the board write four vowel phonemes and ten consonants. Arrange students into teams and challenge them to come up with as many words as they can, using the vowel combinations and consonants on the board. Allot a certain amount of time in which to do this.

The winners are the team who comes up with the highest number of words. Round off by taking feedback from the students and 'rewarding' the winners in whatever way you think is appropriate.

Playgroup

Read the text below and see if you can find words using their long and short vowel sounds. Make a list of them at the bottom of the page.

From the age of two years a child may go to a playgroup. Going to playgroup helps children to develop their social skills, get used to other carers and take part in a variety of activities. They have experience of a different type of routine, working and playing with other children and they get used to their parents leaving and coming back for them.

LONG   **SHORT**

The long and the short of it

Try and identify the long and short vowel sounds in the words listed below. The vowels in each word are written in bold and underlined. Be careful – there are some words with long and short vowel sounds! (One has already been done for you)

s<u>o</u>ngs   <u>a</u>llergies   m<u>u</u>s<u>i</u>c   b<u>a</u>by

cl<u>o</u>thes   r<u>e</u>sp<u>e</u>ct   <u>i</u>m<u>a</u>ginative   c<u>u</u>ts

<u>e</u>m<u>o</u>tion<u>a</u>l   v<u>i</u>r<u>u</u>s<u>e</u>s   h<u>e</u>lper   t<u>i</u>me

v<u>a</u>lues   c<u>u</u>ltures   c<u>o</u>llege

WORD	SHORT VOWEL	WORD	LONG VOWEL
s<u>o</u>ngs	o		

HANDOUT 21

Long vowel phonemes

Some vowel phonemes are made up of more than one letter.

Sometimes it is two letters as in 'or'.

Sometimes it is three letters as in 'air'.

Below is a list of the most common ways of spelling them:

- 'air' as in fair
- 'are' as in care
- 'ere' as in there
- 'ear' as in bear
- 'or' as in sport
- 'oor' as in door
- 'aw' as in raw
- 'au' as in taught
- 'ore' as in core
- 'ear' as in hear
- 'ea' as in spread

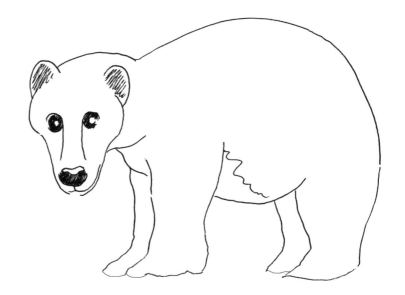

Rw/E2.2
Ww/
E2.1, 2

Common vowel phonemes

Vowel phonemes are sounds in words that are represented by:

*A single vowel as in d**o**g*
*A combination of vowels as in **ea**ch*
*A combination of a vowel and a consonant as in c**ar**d*

The common vowel phonemes are:

- oo made by **u** (p**u**ll) and **oo** (g**oo**d)
- ar made by **ar** (c**ar**)
- oy made by **oi** (**oi**l) and **oy** (b**oy**)
- ow made by **ow** (c**ow**) and **ou** (s**ou**nd)

 ou

You can see by these examples that some sounds can be made in more than one way. This is one of the things that makes the English language so hard to grasp!

Can you think of any more words using the vowel phonemes listed above?

SESSION 3

Outline

In this session you will be working on some spelling strategies with your students and looking at some more vowel phonemes, reinforcing much of the work done in the previous session.

Activities

Activity 1   Introduction

Explain to students that the reason why we spend so much time on spelling patterns and strategies is that by using them and familiarising ourselves with them we reduce the chances of making spelling errors.

- Spend some time recapping vowel phonemes covered during the previous session.
- Point out that at this level there are two more sets of vowel phonemes to work on, in addition to the ones they looked at in Session 2.

Activity 2   Focus exercise

- Give out copies of Handout 23, 'More "phlipin" vowel phonemes!' and go through the different sound and letter combinations with the students, inviting them to come up with other words containing these combinations.

- In pairs, ask students to work their way through Activity Sheet 14, 'Making words'. You might like to start them off with an example, e.g. replacing 'p' with 'h' to turn 'pair' into 'hair'. At the end of the exercise ask students to feed back their suggestions to the rest of the group.
- Tell the group that now you have done quite a bit of work on vowel phonemes together they should be starting to recognise and use them in their own writing. As an extension to the exercise above, ask them to add more words containing the phonemes to the short and long vowel sounds section in their Workbook. This will need to be reviewed on a regular basis.

Activity 3   Explanation

Tell students that you are now going to move on to spelling strategies. One of the best ways to learn how to spell words is to USE them again and again in our writing and reading and when we speak to one another. The more familiar words become, the easier they are to spell.

Point out that there are a lot of words that students already know just by looking at them. These are called 'sight vocabulary' and are words you know without having to work them out. To reinforce this idea ask students to have a go at the exercise in Activity Sheet 15, 'Sign words' and afterwards see how many different suggestions they have managed to come up with.

Activity 4 Group discussion

- Explain to the students that the next step is to build up their sight vocabulary. The best way to do this is to work on using and spelling the words correctly. Tell the group that you are going to look at some words of advice on learning to spell. Give out copies of Handout 24, 'Tips for spelling' and spend some time discussing each point in turn. Has anyone tried any of these (or other) strategies to help them improve their spelling?

- Give out copies of Handout 25, 'Common types of spelling errors' and consider each error in turn, discussing possible ways of avoiding them. During the discussion ask if anyone in the group recognises any of the errors as being something they struggle with.

- Distribute copies of Handout 26, 'Ways to improve your spelling' to the class and explain that these are just some of the strategies that the group will be looking at in forthcoming sessions.

- Give out copies of Handout 27, 'Strategies to help improve your spelling' and go through the various methods with the students. It is worth spending some time on this and giving students an opportunity to try the strategies for themselves.

Activity 5 Focus exercise

Ww/
2.1, 2
Rw/E2.3

Now give students a chance to try some of these spelling strategies out. Give a short spelling quiz (don't call it a test – the very word 'test' strikes fear into some people!), following the method below:

- Read out seven or eight words from a childcare book, including one or two that could be quite difficult to spell. Ask the students to write these down individually.

- When you have called out all of the words, write the correct spellings on the board so that the students can check their own work. Ask for feedback on which ones people made errors with (be careful here, some people will be reluctant to talk openly about their errors and should not be pressured to do so). Choose a couple of words that several people got wrong and write these on the board. Demonstrate some of the spelling strategies using these 'error words' as a basis.

- Give students some time to look through Handout 27 again and choose a couple of strategies they would like to try. They should then concentrate on one or two of their error words at a time and use the chosen strategies to practise spelling them correctly.

- Once you feel you have spent an adequate amount of time on this, repeat the spelling quiz using the same words as last time. As well as helping you judge how effective these strategies have been, it will give individual students an idea of which strategies work best for them.

- Discuss results:

  - Was there any difference from the last quiz?
  - Why or why not?
  - Did the chosen strategies help? Why or why not?
  - Will they try another strategy?

- Ask students to record their error words in the spelling section of their Workbook (pp. 71–88) and practise them before the next session. Remind them that a few minutes every day is much better than an hour once a week!

Activity 6   Group discussion

End the session by telling the students that you would like to do a 'spelling quiz' every session and discuss how they feel about this. Explain that the quiz will comprise no more than seven or eight words at a time and will include a mixture of childcare words and high-frequency words. Words that people have spelt incorrectly in previous quizzes will also be included.

Experience has shown that students are very receptive to these regular quizzes and they do get to the stage where they will remind you about them! They enjoy keeping track on their progress and look forward to seeing how many spellings they can get right, or even nearly right! Praise and encouragement are important here. While using 'well done' and 'good try' stickers often works well with younger students, mature students might prefer a written comment.

Calling the exercise a 'quiz' rather than a 'test' makes it less intimidating for learners. Some might consider this 'softly, softly' approach to be a little childish, if not patronising, but many people coming into FE with poor literacy skills have missed out at school for some reason and have low self-esteem and little confidence, especially when it comes to spelling. This whole process needs to be done gently.

In essence, improving spelling seems to be about building a person's confidence to 'have a go', to make mistakes without feeling foolish and to focus on improvement rather than failure – on what they can do rather than what they cannot.

More 'phlipin' vowel phonemes!

The sounds *air, or, er, ear* and *ea* are all vowel phonemes – that is, phonemes with a vowel in them.

These are the different ways they can be spelt:

The sound of **air**
- air as in pair
- are as in scare
- ere as in there
- ear as in wear

The sound of **or**
- or as in for
- oor as in floor
- aw as in yawn
- au as in taught
- ore as in more
- oar as in board

The sound of **er**
- er as in serve
- ir as in fir
- ur as in fur

The sound of **ear**
- ear as in fear

The sound of **ea**
- ea as in tread

Can you think of any more words with these combinations in them?

© June Green (2003) *Basic Skills for Childcare – Literacy*. Published by David Fulton Publishers Ltd.

Even more vowel phonemes!

Remember the five vowels?

a   e   i   o   u

There are a lot of letter combinations that make these vowel phonemes.

The sound of 'a'

- a...e as in <u>ga</u>me and n<u>a</u>m<u>e</u>
- ay as in pl<u>ay</u> and cr<u>ay</u>on
- ai as in p<u>ai</u>nt and tr<u>ai</u>n

The sound of 'e'

- ee as in b<u>ee</u> and sl<u>ee</u>p
- ea as in <u>ea</u>sels and b<u>ea</u>ker

The sound of 'i'

- ie as in l<u>ie</u>
- i...e as in t<u>i</u>m<u>e</u> and k<u>i</u>t<u>e</u>
- igh as in h<u>igh</u> and light
- y as in fl<u>y</u> and cry

The sound of 'o'

- oa as in b<u>oa</u>t and t<u>oa</u>st
- o...e as in h<u>o</u>m<u>e</u> and cl<u>o</u>s<u>e</u>
- ow as in sh<u>ow</u> and kn<u>ow</u>

The sound of 'u'

- u...e as in t<u>u</u>n<u>e</u> and J<u>u</u>n<u>e</u>
- oo as in m<u>oo</u>n and sp<u>oo</u>n
- ew as in fl<u>ew</u> and kn<u>ew</u>
- ue as in bl<u>ue</u> and tr<u>ue</u>

Making words

By changing the letters (apart from the vowel phonemes) how many words can you make using the same vowel phoneme?
(Write your suggestions below each word)

p<u>ai</u>r   c<u>a</u>re   h<u>er</u>

f<u>ir</u>   f<u>ur</u>   tr<u>ai</u>n

b<u>ite</u>   gr<u>ow</u>   kn<u>ew</u>

<u>ea</u>sels   tr<u>ue</u>   f<u>ew</u>

Sign words

Below are some words that you will see daily when you are out and about. The more you see them and say them the easier they become to recognise and spell.

What do they say and where might you see them? (Write your answers below each one)

FOR SALE

LIFTS

BEWARE OF THE DOG!

lunch

Wash

Bus

WET PAINT!

HOT!

COLD

closed

Tips for spelling

No matter how you try to improve your spelling, if you don't work at it, it won't happen!

So here are some tips before you start:

✓ Improving spelling takes time and focus.

✓ It needs to be done in small manageable chunks.

✓ It takes time and commitment.

✓ You have to practise it regularly.

✓ A short time every day is better than one long session a week.

✓ The more you try to memorise spellings the easier they become to remember.

✓ Not all words can be worked out from the letter sounds – visual strategies may be needed too.

✓ Writing will help you to spell. The more you write, the more you use and see the words; the more you use and see them, the more familiar they will become.

It might sound like there's a lot of work to be done, BUT IT'S WORTH IT!

LET'S GO FOR IT!!

HANDOUT 25

Common types of spelling errors

Type of error	Example	Tips
Right sound but wrong letters	menshun – *mention*	* Keep lists of similarly spelt words * Look at them regularly
Didn't use a spelling rule	comeing – *coming* 'drop the e'	* Get to know the rules you need or often forget
Missing letters Extra letters	missin – *missing* extrah – *extra*	* Highlight or mark the bits you get confused about
Wrong word	two much work – *too* much work	* Use memory tricks to learn when to use each one
Reversed letters	Firday – *Friday*	* Look at the difficult parts of the word and sound them out or underline them
Spelling it the way you say it	somefing – *something*	* Keep lists of your typical errors and get to know your weak spots – it's easier to avoid them

Your errors are a great resource to help you improve your spelling.

If you know and understand why you make mistakes it will help you to:

- know what to look for when proof-reading your work
- identify areas that you need to work on
- take control of your spelling.

© June Green (2003) *Basic Skills for Childcare – Literacy*. Published by David Fulton Publishers Ltd.

Ways to improve your spelling

✓ Look, say, cover, write, check

✓ Finding words within words

✓ Breaking words down into syllables

✓ Working on letter/sound patterns (you've done plenty of that!)

✓ Tracing the shape of the word with your finger

✓ Word games, e.g. hangman, crosswords and word-searches

✓ Using a dictionary

✓ Memory tricks, e.g. 'see the lie in believe'

HANDOUT 27

Strategies to help improve your spelling

There are quite a few different methods you can use to improve your spelling. Try these out and see which ones suit you.

1. LOOK, SAY, COVER, WRITE, CHECK

- Look at the word

- Say the word

- Cover the word

- Write the word

- Check your spelling

2. FINDING WORDS WITHIN WORDS

Sometimes people get into a muddle over which form of a word to use, e.g. *here* or *hear*.

Try this:

I h<u>ear</u> with my <u>ear</u>   I came <u>here</u> from t<u>here</u>

3. BREAKING WORDS DOWN INTO SYLLABLES (see 'Glossary' in your Workbook for a reminder of *syllable*)

Children = chil/dren   nursery = nur/se/ry

Did you notice that each syllable contains a vowel? They get everywhere don't they!

4. USING PHONEMES

Remember phonemes? You looked at some earlier on. They are the smallest meaningful unit of sound in a word, for example:

C/A/T   CH/I/LD   B/OO/K   P/L/AY

Each part of these words is a phoneme. Some are made by one letter and others by more than one. Here's how phonemes can help you spell.

- If you can say a word but are not sure how to spell it try this:

    1. Say the word slowly one phoneme at a time
    2. As you say each phoneme write it down – nine times out of ten you'll get it right!

- If you come across a word you are unfamiliar with when you are reading try this:

    1. Break it down into phonemes
    2. Say each phoneme, blend them together and you should have it!

5. INITIAL LETTER COMBINATIONS

These are good clues for spelling. For example:

- 'Child' begins with 'ch', a vowel sound always follows a 'ch' sound.
- Once you can spell 'child' you only need to add the suffix 'ren' to make it into 'children'.

The more you become familiar with initial letter combinations it becomes easier to build the word as you have something to build on.

HANDOUT 27 continued

---

6. TRACING THE WORD WITH YOUR FINGER

Tracing the word with your finger helps you to remember the shape of the letters when you write them.

7. LOOKING AT THE SHAPE OF A WORD

When you look at the outline shape of a word it can give you clues about the letters in the word. Some letters are tall and others are short. This can be a useful 'memory jogger' when you use the word again.

Have a go at making the shape of these words:

much   here   before   little   for   look

day   sugar   month   top   up

Some of them have quite distinctive shapes, don't they.

OTHER THINGS YOU CAN DO ARE:

*   Use letter tiles to spell out the words – you can move them around until you get it right.
*   Make up a saying to help you remember how to spell a word you find tricky. Say, for example, you keep including an extra 'f' in 'professional' (proffessional) you might come up with the phrase 'one fish, two swimmers' (one 'f', two 's's).
*   Word-searches – you need to keep looking at the word you are trying to find because this will make it familiar to you and you'll eventually recognise it in the search.
*   Making words from one big word. Try this: how many words can you make from the word 'DEVELOPMENT'?
*   Sometimes it is only part of a word you have problems with. If this happens write the word on a card, writing the difficult part in a different colour, and keep looking at it. When you need to use the word try and visualise it on the card.
*   Association – remembering where you saw or used the word before, and the context in which you saw or used it, can often help you remember how to spell it the next time you need to use it.

SESSION 4

Outline

In previous sessions students have done a lot of vocabulary work that will help them with spelling and understanding words. The focus of this session moves on to look at the different beginnings and endings that can be used to change words and introduces the concept of tenses.

> For this session you will need:
>
> • A selection of newspaper and magazine articles, which are based on past or present events. (It would be a good idea to photocopy these for Session 5 – in case students forget to bring their work along with them.)

Activities

Activity 1   Introduction

• After giving students a general outline of the session (see above), write the word 'play' on the board and ask the group what it means. Responses will usually be something along the lines of 'it's something that children do'.

• Beneath this add the words 'playing' and 'played'. Explain that by adding 'ing' to the word 'play' we have made it into its 'present tense' – something that is happening now. Explain that by adding 'ed' to the word 'play' we have made it into its 'past tense' – something that happened before now.

Activity 2   Idea storm

Ask students to think of some activities children do at placement and try adding 'ing' and 'ed' to them. Take suggestions and write them on the board.

Point out to students that 'ing' and 'ed' are very common endings and that they will see them a great deal.

Activity 3   Focus exercise

Give out copies of Activity Sheet 16, 'Student log' and ask students to have a go at the exercise. Take feedback once they have completed the activity.

Activity 4   Focus exercise

Start by asking students to complete the exercise on Activity Sheet 17, 'Happening or happened?' Once they are all happy with this, invite the students to write a few sentences about something they did before today and something they are going to do either later today or sometime soon. Remind them about spelling and what they have just learnt about tenses.

This is a good opportunity for you to wander round the group and get a sense of how individuals are coping with spelling and the concept of tense.

Tell students to make sure they bring this writing to the next session.

Activity 5   Paired discussion

- Divide students into pairs and give out the newspaper and magazine articles you collected before the start of the session.
- Tell students to read through and discuss the articles with their partner, identifying the past and present tenses as they go through.
- Take feedback once everyone has finished. Did the students find the activity easy or difficult?
- Tell students to make sure they bring these articles to the next session.

Ww/E2.2
Rw/E2.3

Student log

Read through the passage below and highlight the past and present tenses. Make a list of each.

WEDNESDAY

Today the children are painting the Christmas decorations they made out of clay yesterday. They really enjoyed using the clay yesterday.

The children are using Christmas colour paints – red, gold, green and silver. When they have painted them they are going to put glitter on them and a thread to hang them with.

I am helping the children with the activity. Yesterday I helped some of them with their clay modelling.

PRESENT   PAST

Ww/E2.2
Rw/E2.3

ACTIVITY SHEET 17

Happening or happened?

Look at the sentences below.

Which ones are written in the past and which are written in present tense? (Write your answers alongside)

- The children played noisily.

- The school is having a summer fair today.

- The nursery nurse is changing the baby's nappy.

- Samreen went to India in the summer.

- Ros had prepared lots of activities for the children to do.

- Margaret is reading a story to the children.

- Noreen listened carefully to her tutor.

- Isma told her tutor that she enjoys working with babies.

SESSION 5

Outline

This session is loosely divided into two parts: in the first, students will be doing some more work on changing words and will be introduced to verbs and singular and plural words. In the second, students will familiarise themselves with dictionaries and their uses.

For this session you will need:

- Copies of the newspaper and magazine articles from the last session, just in case students forget to bring their own copies back.
- Enough dictionaries for each student to work from individually during this session.

Activities

Activity 1 Introduction

- Recap past and present tenses covered in the last session. Ask the group to try to recall some of the words that they came across when looking for past and present tense words in the articles at the end of Session 4. Write a list of these words on the board.
- See if the students can spot what type of words these are – what is common about them?
- Point out that these words are 'action' words – they are telling you what someone or something is doing. These sorts of words are called VERBS. Explain that there are different kinds of verbs and that the students will be looking at them in a later session.

Activity 2 Discussion/idea storm

- Give out copies of Handout 28, 'Vibrant verbs' and explain that 'vibrant' is a good way to describe verbs because they are so full of energy and action!
- Can students think of any verbs to do with children? List their suggestions on the board. You could give them the following examples to start them off:

playing   climbing   singing   painting

- Point out that verbs are very important: there is one in every sentence. In fact, they are at the heart of every sentence.
- Invite the students to look through the newspaper and magazine articles used in Session 4 and to pick out the verbs in the sentences. They might like to work in their original pairs for this exercise.
- Take feedback once the students have finished. How do they feel they have coped with the work on verbs done in this activity?

Activity 3 Focus exercise

Working from the articles used in the previous activity, ask students to read through the text they have been using and list any unfamiliar words. Tell them that they will have an opportunity to look these up in a dictionary activity (Activity 5) later on in the session.

Activity 4   Explanation/idea storm

- Remind students that in the last session the group looked at how to change the tense of words. Do a brief recap using two or three words as examples.
- Explain that another way of changing words is to change them from singular (one) to plural (more than one). This is done by adding 's' or 'es' to the end of the singular word, for example:

'student' (singular) + 's' = 'students' (plural)

'match' (singular) + 'es' = 'matches' (plural)

- Put students into pairs and give each pair a blank sheet of flipchart. Ask them to divide the sheet into two columns, one headed 'singular' and the other headed 'plural'. Each pair is to idea storm as many words as possible that can be changed from singular to plural.
- When the students have finished, put the flipcharts around the room and discuss what is on them as a group.

Activity 5   Group discussion/focus exercise

- Explain to students that they are now going to do some dictionary work. For this activity each student will need a dictionary and the list of unfamiliar words from the magazine and newspaper articles they were using previously.
- Hold a discussion around the questions 'What is a dictionary?' and 'What can we use it for?' Start by explaining two key points:

  1. A dictionary is a book that lists words in alphabetical order and explains what they mean.
  2. A dictionary can be used to look up the meaning or check the spelling of a word.

- Give out copies of Handout 29, 'What can we use a dictionary for?' and Handout 30, 'How to use a dictionary' and go through them with the students.

- Tell students to look at their unfamiliar words from the articles they have been working on and to try and find the meaning of some of them using their dictionary. They can do this as individuals or in pairs. When they have found the meanings tell them to write them into the dictionary section of their Workbook (pp. 90–115).

Activity 6   Focus exercise

End the session with a game entitled 'How quick can you find me?' Put students into pairs. Call out a word and see who can find it first in the dictionary. Do this a few times, making sure there is plenty of emphasis on the fun aspect of the game!

Vibrant verbs

- A verb is a word that describes an action.

- A verb tells you what someone or something is doing.

- Verbs can be more than one word, e.g. _will go_ is a verb.

- Verbs in the past tense tell us about something that has happened or what someone did, e.g. 'the students _went_ to placement last week'.

- Verbs in the future tense tell us about something that will happen or what someone will do, e.g. 'the students _will go_ to placement next week'.

- Verbs in the present tense tell us about what is happening now or what someone is doing at this very moment, e.g. 'the students _are_ at placement this week'.

What can we use a dictionary for?

A dictionary is a book that lists words in alphabetical order and explains their meaning or meanings.

A dictionary gives information about:

➤ the type of word that it is, e.g. verb, noun, etc.

➤ how to say it

➤ other words that come from it or belong to it

➤ other forms of the word and how to use it.

A dictionary can be used to find out the meaning of the word, to check how to spell it or to find another word to use.

How to use a dictionary

We do not have to start at the beginning of a dictionary to find out about a word. As you know, the words are listed in alphabetical order. At the top of each page you will find the first and last word that are on the page, for example:

introduce – invent

This tells you the range of words you will find on the page. All the words will begin with 'in' and the third letter will be t, u or v. When you want to look for a word:

1. Find the section with words that begin with the same letter as the word you are looking for.
2. Find the page with words that have the same first and second letter as your word.
3. Do the same for the first, second and third letter and so on until you find your word. (You can usually find it by the third letter!)

The entry for the word you are looking for will be set out something like this:

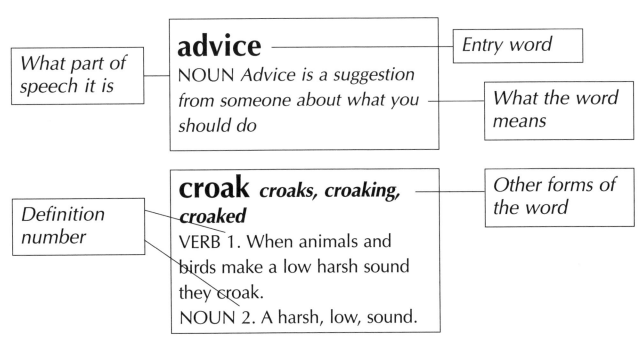

Once you've found your word you can check the spelling, the meaning and find out what part of speech it is. Dictionaries contain a wealth of information!

SESSION 6

Outline

In this session students will be examining a range of texts, reading them for sense and working on their Speaking and Listening skills in the process. They will also have an opportunity to revise the areas covered in Sessions 4 and 5 – tenses, singular and plural endings and verbs – and in addition will be introduced to two new parts of speech – nouns and adjectives.

> For this session you will need:
>
> • Copies of some different texts of varying complexity. A range of newspapers, magazines, textbooks and childcare magazines would be best.

Activities

Activity 1 | Introduction

• Arrange students into twos and give each pair a selection of texts. Ask them to each choose a text to read.

• Hand out copies of Activity Sheet 18, 'What's this all about?' and tell the students to complete the exercise. Explain that they will be asked to tell their partner what the article is about and what led them to this conclusion as they have read it. Their partner should have a couple of questions ready to ask. Although it is probably best not to put a time limit on this activity, don't let it drag on for too long. Have some games etc. ready for people who finish the exercise quickly. This is a good opportunity for you to get a feel for the students' Speaking and Listening skills and to identify any weaknesses.

Rw/E2.3
Rs/E2.2

• Once the exercise is complete ask students, working in pairs, to read through one of their articles and:

   – Identify the verbs(s)
   – Say whether they are past, present or future tense
   – Identify any plurals.

Activity 2 | Explanation/idea storm

• Explain to the students that they are now going to look at a new part of speech. Remind them about the verbs they learnt in Session 5. Recap what they are and ask learners to give you some examples.

• The next part of speech that you are going to look at are NOUNS. Nouns are words that are used for naming things, for example people, places, animals and objects or things. Your own name is a noun, the word 'mouse' is a noun, so is 'London' and 'ladder'.

• Give out copies of Handout 31, 'Naming nouns' and go through it with the students.

• When students are happy with what they've learnt so far about nouns, put them into pairs and give each pair a blank sheet of flipchart. Ask them to idea storm some examples of each kind of noun and to write these down on their sheet of paper.

- When they have finished coming up with suggestions display the sheets of flipchart around the room and discuss them as a group. Ask the students to find the 'Parts of speech' section in their workbooks (p. 124) and to write down some examples of nouns from the flipcharts dotted around the room. You'll be using these 'noun' flipcharts again when you look at adjectives in Activity 4, so put them in a safe place at the end of the activity.

Activity 3 Focus exercise

As an extension to Activity 2 and to reinforce their understanding of nouns, students should be given copies of Activity Sheet 19, 'Now try these!' and asked to complete the exercise. Take feedback once the students have finished the activity.

Activity 4 Explanation/idea storm

- Tell students that they will now be learning about another part of speech – ADJECTIVES. Adjectives are closely linked to nouns. They are words we use to describe nouns, for example '*small* mouse', '*busy* London'.
- Give out copies of Handout 32, 'Adaptable adjectives' and go through it with the students. When you have finished discussing the differences between the two passages, see if the learners can complete the activity at the bottom of the handout.
- Next ask the group to idea storm some words that may be adjectives. List their suggestions on the board/flipchart. Arrange the students into pairs and tell them to look up each of these words, checking that they are adjectives and finding out what they mean. (Remind students about the dictionary work they did in the previous session.)
- Take out the 'nouns' flipcharts from Activity 2 and display them around the room. Ask students to suggest some adjectives to add to each of the nouns.
- When this is done, ask the students to work together in twos and give each pair a selection of nouns and adjectives. Ask them to come up with a sentence for each, writing the noun, adjective and verb in a different coloured pen. (Alternatively students could highlight them in a different colour.)
- Finish off by discussing the sentences with each pair and/or as a group.

Activity 5 Focus exercise/explanation

Give out copies of Activity Sheet 20, 'Using adjectives' and explain to students that adjectives can be used for purposes of description and to express feelings when we write. Tell them that you would like each of them to write two or three sentences about something they enjoyed and two or three more about something they disliked. They should use adjectives in their writing.

When they have finished, take the sheets in for marking. Explain to students that they have now covered three parts of speech – verbs, nouns and adjectives. Speech and writing are made up of different types of words (parts of speech) and the more they know, understand and use these the better their writing will be and the more interesting their reading will become.

Activity 6 Focus exercise

End the session by giving out copies of Activity Sheet 21, 'More sign words' and Activity Sheet 22, 'More high-frequency words'. Depending on how much time you have left you might choose to do both activities orally as a class, going through the words listed on both sheets and discussing which are verbs, nouns and adjectives and where you could see the sign words on Activity Sheet 21.

Alternatively you could ask students to complete the exercises in time for the next session. In this case ask them to write their answers below each sign word on Activity Sheet 21 and to use a different coloured pen to highlight each type of word (verb/noun/adjective) on Activity Sheet 22.

ACTIVITY SHEET 18

Rt/
E2.2, 3, 4
SLlr/
E2.1, 3

What's this all about?

You are going to tell your partner what the article you have chosen is about. Here are some pointers for you:

1. What is your article about?

    - Is it about something that has happened, will happen or is happening now?
    - Is it about something that has been done, will be done or is being done now?
    - Is it about what someone has done, will do or is doing now?

2. What clues can you find in the headlines, pictures, dates, etc.?

3. What is this article trying to do? (Explain, persuade, inform, entertain or instruct?)

4. Where do you think it came from? (A newspaper, magazine, TV guide or junk mail?)

5. What will you tell your partner about the article? Make yourself some notes.

HANDOUT 31

Naming nouns

NOUNS are words used for naming things, for example a person, a place, an animal or a thing:

- Person – Gail
- Place – Birmingham
- Animal – hamster
- Thing – computer

There are four kinds of noun:

1. *Proper nouns* – used to name a particular person, place or thing, e.g. Mexico, Monday, Bushra. Proper nouns always start with a capital letter.
2. *Common nouns* – used to name a kind of person or thing, e.g. boy, day, children.
3. *Collective nouns* – used to name a group or collection of people or things, e.g. team, gang.
4. *Abstract nouns* – used to name things that cannot be seen or heard, e.g. sleep, wind.

Linked very closely to nouns are PRONOUNS. These are words that are used to refer to a person or thing without using its name. They can be used in place of nouns when we want to avoid repeating words, which makes our writing sound clumsy. Take a look at this:

'When Noreen got high grades for her child observations, Noreen was very happy.'

Sounds a bit clumsy, doesn't it? Try this instead:

'When Noreen got high grades for her child observations, she was very happy.'

Sounds better, doesn't it!

Now try these!

Find the nouns in the sentences below. Don't forget proper nouns need capital letters.

✻ It is important to wind babies after feeding them.

✻ Lynsey did not like the Unit 4 assignment.

✻ Children learn how to socialise with others at nursery.

✻ When Rachael's mum leaves Rachael at nursery, Rachael gets upset.

✻ It is important to introduce new foods one at a time when weaning babies.

Is there anywhere you can replace a noun with a pronoun?

HANDOUT 32

Adaptable adjectives

Adjectives are words that:

* can be used to give more information to readers and listeners
* give us detail about nouns
* help us to describe people, places, feelings, objects, etc.

Have a look at these two pieces of writing. What's the difference between them?

The children went to see Father Christmas. While they were there they had a good time. They told us about seeing Father Christmas and the presents he had given them.

The excited children went to see Father Christmas. While they were there they had a really good time. They told us all about seeing Father Christmas and the lovely presents he had given them.

The second piece of writing sounds fun and vibrant. It tells us that the children were excited about the trip and how much they enjoyed it!

ACTIVITY
Underline the words you think are adjectives in the second passage.

Using adjectives

Write a few sentences about each of the following:

✳ Something you have enjoyed, e.g. a book, a visit, a film, something you have seen, etc.

✳ Something you have not enjoyed (as above).

Use adjectives in your writing to give it feeling and description.

Rw/E2.2

ACTIVITY SHEET 21

More sign words

Remember the sign words you looked at in Session 3? Here are a few others.

What do they say and where would you see them?

pull

TELEPHONE

Bar

push

Way

private

closed

open

More high-frequency words

Here are some more high-frequency words to add to the others:

after	gave	play	am
going	read	away	green
round	because	head	saw
black	house	should	bring
keep	soon	don't	left
tell	far	long	thing
fell	may	time	fly
Mr	under	once	walk

SESSION 7

Outline

The object of this session will be to introduce students to compound sentences. As well as reinforcing their understanding of the different parts of speech learnt in previous sessions, students will also revisit work they did on simple sentences and punctuation in Entry Level One.

For this session you will need:

- Different coloured highlighter pens.
- Recipes or instructions written on card and cut up into individual steps. Each recipe/set of instructions should be placed in its own envelope.
- Sets of sentences and linking words for a paired activity (as many sets as there are pairs in your group). Choose some compound sentences from childcare books and children's stories, e.g. 'Young children pick up infections easily so it is important that early years settings are as hygienic as possible.' Take out the linking word and split each compound sentence into two simple sentences, e.g. 'Young children pick up infections easily' (as one sentence) and 'It is important that early years settings are as hygienic as possible' (as another sentence). Write each simple sentence on a separate piece of card and put about five sets of split compound sentences into an envelope with a selection of linking words (including those from the original compound sentences).

Activities

Activity 1 **Introduction**

Start by recapping simple sentences and punctuation of a sentence (covered in Entry Level One).

Activity 2 **Focus exercise**

In order to judge how much information students have managed to retain, ask them to write some simple sentences about:

- the weather
- college
- their placement.

See if they can then come up with some simple sentences that:

- ask a question
- make an exclamation.

Finish off by asking them to highlight the verbs, nouns and adjectives in these sentences using different coloured pens.

This activity is a good opportunity to evaluate how much students remember/know about sentences, punctuation and the use of different parts of speech, and to identify any problem areas.

Activity 3 Explanation/focus exercise

- Having covered simple sentences in Entry Level One, students are now going to learn about COMPOUND SENTENCES. Explain to students that compound sentences are bigger than simple sentences. They are made up of two or more simple sentences joined together with conjunctions to make a bigger more complicated sentence. Compound sentences can make your writing flow more smoothly.
- To reinforce these points, give out copies of Handout 33, 'Compound sentences' and Handout 34, 'Linking words' and go through them with the students.
- Arrange students into twos and give each pair an envelope of sentences, which you prepared before the start of the session, and Activity Sheet 23, 'Let's get together'. Ask them to complete the exercise on the sheet.

Activity 4 Explanation

As an extension to Activity 3, give out copies of Handout 35, 'It's time for a cuppa!' and go through it with the students. Explain that texts giving instructions and directions use linking words of a certain type. Look at the questions at the bottom of the handout and try to answer them together.

Activity 5 Focus exercise

Give each student a copy of Activity Sheet 24, 'Story time'. There are a number of steps involved in this activity so the whole thing can be quite time consuming. Encourage students to aim to have the planning done and the first draft started by the end of the first session. Give them some time in the next session to finish it.

This activity would be a good opportunity for students to use word processing. The finished stories will look great and will boost students' confidence enormously.

Activity 6 Focus exercise

End the session with a fun team activity. Put students into pairs or small groups and give each pair/group one of the envelopes containing the cut up recipes or instructions, which you prepared before the start of the session. Ask them to put the recipe/instructions together in the right order. Whichever team/pair finishes first and arranges the pieces in the correct order wins!

Rs/
E2.1, 2

HANDOUT 33

Compound sentences

Do you remember simple sentences? These are short sentences with one subject, e.g. *'The student was changing the baby's nappy.'*

Now it's time to move on to COMPOUND SENTENCES!
A compound sentence is made up of two or more simple sentences joined together with a linking word. If you took away the linking words, the sentences would make sense on their own. For example:

'The children were changing for PE <u>and</u> the nursery nurse was trying to help them.'

If you took away the linking word <u>and</u> the two sentences would make sense on their own:

- *The children were changing for PE.*
- *The nursery nurse was trying to help them.*

Let's look at the compound sentence again:

The <u>children</u> were changing for PE and the <u>nursery nurse</u> was trying to help them.

1. This sentence has two <u>subjects</u>.
2. This sentence has two verbs.

Linking words

Here is a list of 'linking words' that you can use to:

- link simple sentences together to make compound sentences
- link instructional text, e.g. recipes

and

however

but

then

so

also

when

because

therefore

ACTIVITY SHEET 23

Let's get together

In the envelope you have been given you will find:

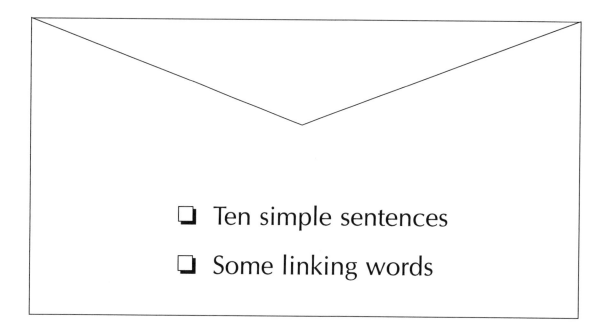

❏ Ten simple sentences

❏ Some linking words

Using some of the linking words, join the simple sentences together to make five compound sentences.

BE CAREFUL! There are more linking words than sentences – so you'll have to work out which linking word fits which sentence.

If you get stuck, look back at Handout 33, 'Compound sentences'.

Rs/E2.1
Rt/E2.1

 It's time for a cuppa!

In texts that give instructions or directions you will find a particular type of linking word, e.g. 'next', 'after' and 'then'. These are words that put the steps of doing something into the right order. They give details about time, sequence and order, and enable the reader to follow the instructions or directions correctly.

Read the following text:

Put enough water into a kettle <u>then</u> switch it on to boil <u>then</u> put a teabag into a cup. <u>When</u> the water has boiled pour it into the cup, <u>next</u> add some milk. Stir until it looks the right strength for your taste <u>then</u> sit down and enjoy a well-deserved cuppa.

Have a go at answering these questions about the text above:

1. What is the first thing you need to do?

2. What should you do last?

3. What is the third thing you need to do?

4. What is the fifth thing you should do?

Ww/
E2.1, 2, 3
Ws/E2.1,
2, 3, 4
Wt/E2.1

ACTIVITY SHEET 24

Story time

Pick one of these pictures below and write a short story about it for a child. Follow these instructions:

✳ Your story should be about four paragraphs long.

✳ Use nouns, adjectives and verbs.

✳ Use some simple and some compound sentences.

✳ Plan and draft it.

✳ When you are happy, write it out neatly.

✳ When you have finished give the planning sheets, draft copy and final copy to your tutor for marking.

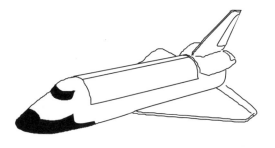

© June Green (2003) *Basic Skills for Childcare – Literacy*. Published by David Fulton Publishers Ltd.

SESSION 8

Outline

In this session students will be exploring a variety of text types, locating information and tracing main events within texts. The activities are intended to reinforce work done in previous sessions on the structure and content of sentences and how this links to meaning.

> For this session you will need:
>
> * Flipchart with the following sentence written at the top of the page:
>
>   *'You need to check how many scoops and how much water is needed for the amount you want to make.'*

Activities

Activity 1 Introduction

* Get the session underway by recapping what was learnt in the previous session about compound sentences and linking words.

Activity 2 Group discussion

Tell the students that they are now going to look at how word order, punctuation and their own knowledge can help them to decipher words and the meaning of text.

Explain that sometimes we read text that we find difficult to understand at first. It might be that there are a lot of unfamiliar words in it, or that it's written in technical language or jargon. People often come up against this when they start a new course. Lots of courses have specialist jargon of their own. Have students ever experienced this? Maybe they came across it when they started the childcare course?

Sometimes there are pointers that can help us to unearth the meaning of a text, for example: `Rs/E2.2, 3, 4` `Rt/E2.4`

* Type of language being used
* Words that are repeated
* Order of the words
* Punctuation
* Relationship between the words
* Titles, sub-headings, captions and headlines
* Pictures and diagrams.

Display the flipchart with the sentence *'You need to check how many scoops and how much water is needed for the amount you want to make'* on it, which you prepared before the start of the session. Explain that it is an extract from a piece of text. Ask the students to consider the following: `Rs/ E2.2, 3` `Rt/E2.2`

* What is the text about?

- What does it mean?
- Does it make sense?
- What type of text did it come from?

Write the following words on the flipchart, below the extract:

- *making babies' formula feeds*
- *first*
- *of milk formula*
- *(manufacturer's instructions)*
- *of formula*

Explain that one of these lines is the title of the article from which the extract is taken. The other four lines contain words that are missing from the extract. Can the students spot the title ('*Making babies' formula feeds*')? This should help them to work out what the text is about. Once they have done this, see if they can slot the words into the extract so that the whole thing makes sense (and relates to the title).

Discuss the following points:

- When students first looked at the sentence all they had were a few non-specific words. The sentence could have been about any number of things.
- When the title was added you had a big clue as to what the text was about.
- The list of words gave you the rest of the information.
- If you look at the list of words, in just one sentence the word '*formula*' appears twice in the text and the word '*milk*' appears once.
- If you link this with the words '*making*' and '*babies*' from the title you can conclude that this sentence came from directions for making up babies' milk formula.

Give students copies of Handout 36, 'Making babies' formula feeds'. Can they find the extract in the text? Does it make more sense now they have the whole article in front of them? Why? What sort of text have they been looking at? (Instructions for making up babies' feeds.)

Activity 3   Focus exercise

Activity Sheets 25–9, 'What's missing? (Texts 1–5)' are all based on a gap-filling exercise and are designed to help you make sure that everyone grasped the work done in the previous activity. Students are given a text in which some words have been missed out and are asked to insert words from a list below the text.

Hand out copies of the five activity sheets and ask the students to work their way through the activities in pairs or small groups. (A copy of the completed texts has been provided for you in Figure 3.3.)

Once the students have finished, check their work and gather feedback on the activity.

Tutor's answers to the 'What's missing?' activities

1. As children get <u>older</u> they build a <u>picture</u> of themselves. This is called <u>self-image</u>. It is built through reactions of <u>others</u> to them, through <u>praise</u> and <u>love</u> from parents and carers.

2. When planning <u>activities</u> and <u>games</u> for children we need to know their <u>age</u> and <u>stage</u> of development. We need to <u>know</u> this so that we can <u>plan</u> the <u>activity</u> to meet their <u>needs</u>.

3. At six to nine months of age, <u>babies</u> are being <u>weaned</u>. They may want to <u>feed</u> themselves. <u>Carers</u> can encourage this by giving them a spoon to <u>hold</u> while <u>feeding</u> them.

4. <u>Young</u> children have to <u>learn</u> to <u>sit</u> still and listen to <u>others</u> e.g. during story time at nursery<u>. T</u>here are a lot of activities that can encourage them to build this <u>skill.</u> <u>T</u>hese include <u>board</u> games, puppet shows, circle <u>time</u> and <u>meal</u> times.

5. <u>Babies</u> grow quickly, especially during the first few <u>months. T</u>hey also need lots of changes of <u>clothes</u>. It is important that clothes are the right <u>size</u> and made of suitable <u>material</u> because they are growing so <u>quickly</u>.

Figure 3.3 Answers to exercises on Activity Sheets 25–9

| Rt/ |
| E2.2, 3, 4 |

Activity 4   Discussion/idea storm

So far the students have done quite a lot of work on sentences. The focus for the remainder of this session (and for part of Session 9) will be on text work.

- Start by discussing the fact that there are lots of different types of text around. We read a lot of them daily and they all have a different purpose.
- See if the students can idea storm some suggestions as to what the different texts we read are designed to do. What purposes do they serve? Suggestions might include: to entertain, inform, instruct/direct, explain, recount/retell.
- Give out copies of Handout 37, 'Text types' and go through it with the students. Have an idea storming session based around the following question: 'Where do we see these types of text when we read?' Suggestions might include:

newspapers	leaflets	recipes
magazines	DIY manuals	instructions for making something
novels	statements	directions for getting somewhere
textbooks	text messages	TV and radio guides
junk mail	personal letters	bills and invoices
posters	business letters	teletext

- Give out copies of Activity Sheet 30, 'Different text types' and ask students to do the exercise. Check the answers together once they have finished. (These have been supplied for you in Figure 3.4.)

Tutor's answers to 'Different text types' activity

1 'Lady V's disaster'
- Recount text
- Magazine

2 'Cuts and grazes'
- Explanation text
- Magazine

3 'Cheating will get you everywhere'
- Persuasive text
- TV magazine

4 'A test to spell the end of dyslexia?'
- Information text
- Newspaper

5 'How to make a shaker'
- Instructional text
- Children's activity sheet

Figure 3.4 Answers to exercise on Activity Sheet 30

HANDOUT 36

Making babies' formula feeds

To make a formula feed for a baby it is important that you follow the instructions below.

The first thing you should do is make sure you have everything ready. You will need enough sterilised feeding bottles, teats and caps for the number of feeds you are going to make, formula powder and scoop, and boiling water.

To make the feeds:

You first need to check how many scoops of milk formula (manufacturers' instructions) and how much water is needed for the amount of formula you want to make.

When you have done this put the correct number of scoops of powder into each bottle, then pour on the correct amount of boiling water. After this put on the teats (upside down) and caps. Next shake the bottles until the formula is thoroughly mixed, leave the bottles to cool and then store in the fridge until they are to be used.

Rs/
E2.2, 3, 4
Rw/E2.2
Ws/
E2.1, 3
Ww/E2.2

ACTIVITY SHEET 25

Text 1

What's missing?

In the text below some words have been missed out. You can find these words in the list at the bottom of the page. Try filling in the gaps with the correct word. There are some simple and some compound sentences.

As children get . . . . . . they build a . . . . . . of themselves. This is called . . . . -. . . . . It is built through reactions of . . . . to them, through . . . . and . . . . from parents and carers.

model   love   photograph

older   self-image

younger   picture   praise

teachers   others

skills   family   self-confidence

Can you think of a title for this text?

ACTIVITY SHEET 26

Rs/
E2.2, 3, 4
Rw/E2.2
Ws/
E2.1, 3
Ww/E2.2

Text 2

What's missing?

In the text below some words have been missed out. You can find these words in the list at the bottom of the page. Try filling in the gaps with the correct word. There are some simple and some compound sentences.

When planning . . . . and . . . . for children we need to know about their . . . . and . . . . of development. We need to . . . . this so that we can . . . . the . . . . to meet their . . . .

meals   play   activities

games   children   age

stage   know   plan

activity   needs   likes

Can you think of a title for this text?

Rs/
E2.2, 3, 4
Rw/E2.2
Ws/
E2.1, 3
Ww/E2.2

ACTIVITY SHEET 27

Text 3

What's missing?

In the text below some words have been missed out. You can find these words in the list at the bottom of the page. Try filling in the gaps with the correct word. There are some simple and some compound sentences.

At six to nine months of age, ... are being . . . . They may want to . . . . themselves. . . . . can encourage this by giving them a spoon to . . . . while . . . . them.

children   babies   chew

feed   encouraging   wash   walk

themselves   carers   weaned   hold

hold   fork   apple   feeding   washing

Can you think of a title for this text?

Rs/
E2.2, 3, 4
Rw/E2.2
Ws/
E2.1, 3
Ww/E2.2

ACTIVITY SHEET 28

Text 4

What's missing?

In the text below some words have been missed out. You can find these words in the list at the bottom of the page. Try filling in the gaps with the correct word. Some punctuation and capital letters have been missed out too – try putting them in. There are some simple and some compound sentences.

. . . . children have to . . . . . to . . . . . still and listen to . . . . e.g. during story time at nursery there are lots of activities that can help to build this . . . . these include . . . . games, puppet shows, circle . . . . . . puppets and . . . . times.

older   younger   young   learn   learning   meal

toilet   bath   stand   sit   others

themselves   encourage   skill

word   board   boxes   time

Can you think of a title for this text?

Rs/
E2.2, 3, 4
Rw/E2.2
Ws/
E2.1, 3
Ww/E2.2

ACTIVITY SHEET 29

Text 5

What's missing?

In the text below some words have been missed out. You can find these words in the list at the bottom of the page. Try filling in the gaps with the correct word. Some punctuation and capital letters have been missed out too – try putting them in. There are some simple and some compound sentences.

. . . . *grow quickly, especially during the first few*

. . . . *they also need* . . . . *of changes of*

. . . . *It is important that clothes are the right*

. . . . *and made of suitable* . . . . *because they*

are growing so . . . .

quickly	babies	children	years
weeks	months	lots	grow
	few	lot clothes	
unimportant	important	urgent	
size	shape	material	growing

Can you think of a title for this text?

© June Green (2003) *Basic Skills for Childcare – Literacy.* Published by David Fulton Publishers Ltd.

HANDOUT 37

Text types

Here's a description of the different types of text that you will come across in your reading.

✳ PERSUASIVE This type of text is used when the writer is trying to change someone's mind. The words and sentences have been chosen to make you think in a different way – to see the writer's point of view. The writer will often use pictures and other visual aids to help persuade you.

✳ RECOUNT This type of writing is used to retell something that has happened, e.g. a newspaper report. The focus of the writing will be a particular person and what happened to them, or an event and what took place. There may be photographs to help tell the story.

✳ EXPLANATION This form of writing is used to tell you how something works or the system for doing something. The language used will be simple and straightforward and written in steps that are continued until the process is complete.

✳ INSTRUCTIONS Instructions are written to tell you how to do something in progressive stages. Instructions will be written in straightforward language and in a series of ordered steps, e.g. a numbered list, bullet pointed list or in text that uses chronological language – first, next and after that...

✳ FICTION Fiction is writing that is based on something that is not real. The style of writing will vary according to the storyline. For example, a romance novel will use language about love and emotions whereas a murder novel will use quite dramatic language about killing and motive.

✳ DISCUSSION This form of writing is used to present different viewpoints, e.g. the effect of TV violence on children. It will contain opinions from both sides of the argument and will be written in simple present tense and in a logical order.

ACTIVITY SHEET 30

Different text types

Have a look at the different texts on this page. What are they and where do you think they came from?

TUESDAY 22 OCTOBER, LONDON

Lady's V's disaster

IT WASN'T HALLOWEEN, BUT Lady Victoria Hervey still decided to put on a scary costume for the Pantene Pro-V Spirit Of Beauty Awards at London's Royal Albert Hall.

With her bony frame, Victoria barely managed to fill out the comic-book catsuit – an outfit that even Christina Aguilera would be ashamed of (probably). Ms Hervey's "best friend", designer Scott Henshall, was responsible for the all-in-one nightmare but we couldn't find out exactly who lent her the dodgy wig. Perhaps Worzel

Gummidge is also a close pal?

While we would usually give sympathy points to those who make an effort, we don't even feel that this "Lady" is worthy of that. She had already w the headache-inducing c at a Versace party earlie month. Perhaps she wa to save a few pounds o dry-cleaning bill. Eithe she didn't get enough the first time she wor

Well here you go, Just this once you ca a whole page dedica You must be *sooo* p

Cuts and grazes

FIRST AID: The main risk with cuts and grazes is infection. If the injury is serious or has dirt in it, check whether you're up-to-date with tetanus jabs and see your doctor. Before dealing with less serious nicks and cuts, wash your hands thoroughly and put on disposable gloves if you have them.

'If the wound is dirty, rinse it lightly under cold, running water or use an antiseptic wipe,' says Dr Lotte Newman, chief medical adviser at St John's Ambulance. 'Pat the wound dry using a gauze swab and cover with a sterile dressing,' she adds.

You can slow down bleeding by raising the injured area above the level of your heart. And forget the old advice that wounds need fresh air to heal – research shows that keeping skin injuries in a moist environment helps them heal faster and reduces scarring by speeding up new skin growth.

Cheating will get you everywhere

Now VIEWPOINT

Not very brave to come forward now, is it, Peter?

Hardly a wannabe model, Nathan's been at it for years

At least Hazel confessed in time to be replaced

Cheats never prosper – or do they? Reality TV shows took another battering this week, with revelations surrounding two more wannabes. Peter Smith from Popstars: The Rivals confessed that he's too old for the show, making him the second person to be disqualified on age grounds. Hazel Kaneswaran was booted off earlier for being over the age limit. Meanwhile, Model Behaviour suffered an embarrassment when it turned out that 'unknown' model Nathan Roberts has been modelling for five years and is on the books of 11 agencies. Why haven't the producers done their homework and checked these finalists out? Is it carelessness or is it because it makes great TV when the cheats are exposed? Might we suggest that Fame Academy finds a way of dramatically losing one of its students? It would do wonders for their ratings.

ACTIVITY SHEET 30 continued

Rt/E2.2
Rs/2.3

A test to spell the end of dyslexia?

By JUDY HOBSON

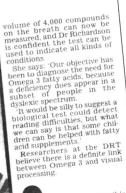

A SIMPLE breath test could lead to children with a predisposition to dyslexia, attention deficit disorder and behavioural problems being identified before they start school and given essential nutrients to feed the brain.

This method of biochemical testing can identify children who are deficient in the Omega 3 essential fatty acids EPA and DHA that are needed by the brain and lacking in today's junk-food diet.

The beauty of the test is that it is non-invasive, and so simple that it can be done on pre-schoolchildren. All a child has to do is to put his mouth around a disposable tube and blow out a single breath for as long as he can.

By measuring the amount of ethane, the breakdown product of Omega 3, the test can show which children and adults could benefit from Omega 3 and Omega 6 supplements — high-grade fish oil and evening primrose.

Dyslexia alone affects at least five per cent of the population. Estimates rise when milder forms are included.

Dyspraxia (poor physical co-ordination) and ADHD (attention-deficit hyperactivity disorder) appear to be at a similar level. Evidence suggests that up to 20 per cent of children may be affected to at least some degree by one or more of these conditions.

THE test, developed by Marion Ross at the Highland Psychiatric Research Foundation, was used on school children for the first time this year in a large-scale study in Co. Durham carried out by the Dyslexic Research Trust and the local education authority.

Until now, the best way to measure for fatty acids has been to take blood samples.

The researcher in charge, Dr

Alex Richardson, Willis Senior Research Fellow at Mansfield College, Oxford, says: 'The test is a follow-on from what doctors were doing 100 years ago.

'When they asked patients to stick out their tongues, they were smelling their breath. What you exude in your breath can tell us a lot about what is going on in the body. Parents of children with dyslexic symptoms often say their child has a funny smell.

'We believe high levels of ethane will help us identify those children using up their Omega 3 fatty acids faster

than oth...
therefor...
supplem...
'If we...
we have...
sive wa...
importa...
with...
before...
read or...
lose co...
'Wha...
better...
ing of...
dren's...
behav...
are p...
really...
With...

volume of 4,000 compounds on the breath can now be measured, and Dr Richardson is confident the test can be used to indicate all kinds of conditions.

She says: 'Our objective has been to diagnose the need for Omega 3 fatty acids, because a deficiency does appear in a subset of people in the dyslexic spectrum.

'It would be silly to suggest a biological test could detect reading difficulties, but what we can say is that some children can be helped with fatty acid supplements.'

Researchers at the DRT believe there is a definite link between Omega 3 and visual processing.

OMEGA 3 is responsible for 30 to 50 per cent of the retina, and without it the retina is unable to send signals to the back of the eye. Studies have shown that when an animal is deprived of Omega 3, it does not develop normal vision.

Many dyslexics complain that when they are trying to read, the letters and words blur or move around, or they get a glare from the text on the page.

How to make a shaker

You will need:

- ☐ A plastic bottle with a screw-on top
- ☐ Dried pasta, peas or rice
- ☐ Non-toxic paint
- ☐ Strong non-toxic glue
- ☐ Decorative bits and pieces

FIRST wash the bottle thoroughly inside and outside and remove any labels. Make sure it is thoroughly dry inside and out.

NEXT put the dried peas/pasta etc. in the bottle — make sure you leave enough room in the bottle for it to move around and make a noise when shaken. Seal the bottle securely.

THEN paint the container with non-toxic paint. When dry, decorate with colourful bits and pieces, stuck on with the strong non-toxic glue.

LASTLY allow it to dry.

You will have an inexpensive, colourful musical instrument suitable for a toddler or young child.

© June Green (2003) *Basic Skills for Childcare – Literacy*. Published by David Fulton Publishers Ltd.

SESSION 9

Outline

Explain to the students that most of the texts you looked at in the previous session came from newspapers, magazines and a tutor's activity book. During this level you have talked about many other sources which contain various sorts of texts. What sort of texts we read will depend on what information we need to find.

For this session you will need:

- A variety of forms, e.g. driving licence, loyalty cards, passport, bus pass, mail order, job application, etc.
- A selection of newspaper and magazine articles that have accompanying pictures, captions and headlines. Cut up the articles and separate the headlines and pictures from the text. Put an assortment of texts and the accompanying pictures, captions, headlines, etc. into envelopes.
- A selection of children's short stories.
- Highlighter pens.

Activities

Activity 1   Introduction

- Start the session off by asking the students to do the exercise on Activity Sheet 31, 'Where should we look?'
- Discuss answers once everyone has completed the exercise.
- Explain that punctuation is something else that helps us to decipher text when we are reading. Just as we use it to give expression to our writing, we can also use it to give tone to our reading. For example, when we see a full stop we know it is the end of a sentence – a *stop here* sign. When we see a question mark we know that the sentence we have read or are reading is asking a question. Give out copies of Handout 38, 'Punctuation and reading' to clarify these points.
- Refer back to Activity Sheet 30, 'Different text types' used at the end of Session 8 and ask students to highlight full stops, question marks and exclamation marks in the text.

Activity 2   Explanation/idea storm

Explain to students that texts contain other elements such as headlines, pictures, captions, subheadings and format, which give us information too.

Ask students to work in pairs for the next activity. Give each pair an envelope of cut up texts, which you prepared before the start of the session. Ask them to match the text to its headline/picture/caption, arranging the various sections of text on the desk in front of them.

Activity 3   Group discussion/focus exercise

Rw/E2.1

Forms are another source of information that we come across regularly in our everyday lives. Although forms usually ask you for information, once you have filled them in they give information to someone else. Discuss the type of information usually requested on forms.

Give students a selection of the forms you collected before the session started. Ask them to have a go at filling different ones in.

Rw/E2.1
Wt/E2.1

Activity 4   Focus exercise

Rt/E2.2
Rs/E2.4
SLlr/
E2.1, 6
SLd/
E2.1, 6

End the session with a reading activity in small groups or pairs. Each person is to pick a story from the selection you have provided. Their task is to read the story (or part of it depending on time, length of story and confidence of reader) to their partner. Readers should use punctuation etc. to add tone to their reading. When each reader has finished, they should have a short discussion about their reading with their partner, how they felt, responses from the listeners, any words that were difficult, and so on.

➤ Congratulations are in order! Students have reached the end of Entry Level Two. Lots of new skills have been learnt and existing ones built on.

WELL DONE TO ALL OF THEM!

130

Where should we look?

Where would you look to find the following information?
(Write your answers below)

1. Telephone number of a local day nursery

2. Information about childhood immunisations

3. Ingredients of a pre-prepared baby's meal

4. Times of a baby and toddler group

5. Activities and outings for children

6. Information on food nutrients

7. Results of a football match

8. Date and times of a film showing

9. Children's physical development

10. Cheap holidays

Punctuation and reading

When you are reading text you will see that it is built up of sentences. Capital letters and punctuation indicate the beginning and ends of sentences – just as you use them in your writing. As with your writing they are used to give tone and information.

1. A full stop (.) means exactly that – 'STOP HERE'.

    This is the end.

2. A question mark (?) means the sentence is asking a question.

    This is the end?

3. An exclamation mark (!) means the sentence is making some sort of exclamation.

    This is the end!

Speaking and Listening activities for Entry Level Two

For this session you will need:

- Short video clips from a variety of programmes such as soaps, documentaries, dramas, chat shows, where people are displaying a variety of feelings; or a video of children during a day at nursery or playgroup, where the children are showing a variety of feelings and emotions.
- Instructions on how to make some sterilising fluid for sterilising babies' bottles, and the equipment to carry out these instructions.
- A video or audiotape of a news programme.

Activity 1

Ask students to work in pairs for this activity. They should start by deciding who will be the instructor and who will be the listener. The instructor then reads out the instructions for making up the steriliser, while the other student carries out the instructions. Reverse roles.

➢ When both students have had a turn at reading out the instructions, discuss how clearly the instructions were given, whether they were easy to follow and which terms were used.

SLlr/E2.5
SLd/
E2.1, 2

Activity 2

Watch the video clips and discuss the following:

- What feelings are being shown?
- How is the feeling expressed by use of verbal language?
- How is the feeling expressed by non-verbal language, e.g. facial expression and body language?

SLlr/E2.6
SLc/
E2.1, 2, 3
SLd/
E2.1, 2

Activity 3

Arrange students into pairs and instruct them to tell each other about what they have been doing at placement recently. They might like to discuss an activity they have done, something that has happened or what they have learnt. They should then ask each other simple questions about placement and give appropriate responses.

SLd/E2.1, 2
SLlr/
E2.2, 3, 4

Activity 4

Watch/listen to the news programme. Afterwards discuss the main points heard in the report, and the language used in relation to different reports. Were there any keywords and phrases that were used?

CHAPTER 4

Entry Level Three

Introduction

The aim of this level is to explore a variety of texts to develop students' word, sentence and text level skills in both reading and writing. Once again students will be building on skills learnt at previous levels, revisiting topics such as the alphabet, tenses, parts of speech, spelling and dictionary work, and moving on to examine specialist vocabulary and new forms of punctuation during more complex sentence work.

The activities in this level are directly related to childcare and are designed to show learners how the skills they have acquired can be used in many different contexts. Students will be learning new reading skills, for example, in an activity in which they use childcare textbooks to do some research for a course assignment.

As usual the sessions are full of ideas for discussion activities and quizzes that can be used to make the learning in this level as interesting and enjoyable as possible.

SESSION 1

Outline

The object of this first session is to give students a general overview of what they will be learning in Entry Level Three and to recap and develop skills learnt in the previous levels. One of the main differences between Entry Level Three and the earlier levels is that here the learning becomes a little more specific: students have a chance to see how various skills relate directly to the context of childcare.

The main focus of this session will be on word work. As well as revising previous work done on the alphabet, prefixes and suffixes, tenses and verbs, students will be introduced to the future tense and will explore specialist vocabulary relating to their course. Spelling is once again covered in an activity in which students are asked to break words down into phonemes and syllables – a strategy introduced in Session 3 of the previous level (see Handout 27, 'Strategies to help improve your spelling' on p. 86). The session also includes a number of opportunities for students to expand their dictionary skills.

For this session you will need:

- A selection of newspaper and magazine cuttings.
- Flipchart with the following written on it:

Prefixes – un dis de re pre
Suffixes – ness less ly ful

- Enough flipchart sheets – each with two verbs written at the top – for students to do a paired activity.
- Enough dictionaries for each student to work from individually during the session.

Activities

Activity 1   Introduction

Start off by discussing with students what they will be working on in Entry Level Three (see Introduction to this chapter). Explain that some of the work, especially in the early sessions, will be based on reinforcing and building on skills covered in Entry Level Two. A short recap of what was covered in the last level should jog a few memories at this point.

Activity 2   Group discussion/explanation

- Can students remember the 'well-used' or 'high-frequency' words and the 'sight vocabulary' they talked about in Entry Levels One and Two? Remind them that these are words that we see and use frequently in day-to-day life. Explain to the group that they are now going to move on to explore some key specialist words – words related to their course and vocation.
- Idea storm words that students have come across on the course or at placement which are related to childcare. Give the group a few examples to start them off: *development* and *assignment* from their course and *crayons* and *collage* at placement.

- Give out copies of Handout 39, 'Specialist words' and go through it with the students. See if they can think of any more words to add to the list.
- Ask students to think back to the prefixes and suffixes they worked on in Session 4 of Entry Level Two. Can they change any of the words on the list by adding a prefix or suffix? (For example, add the suffix 'al' to 'accident' to make 'accidental' and the prefix 'dis' to 'play' to make 'display'.)
- Remind the group that knowing and recognising root words and remembering how to spell prefixes and suffixes are very useful tools for spelling. If you know how to spell 'play' and you know how to spell the suffix 'ing', it stands to reason that you won't have too much trouble spelling 'playing'.

Activity 3 Explanation/focus exercise

- Explain to the students that you are going to work on some more prefixes and suffixes. Briefly recap the work you have previously done on this topic (the time you spend on this will depend on how recently the group did Activity 2).
- Display the flipchart with examples of prefixes and suffixes written on it, which you prepared before the start of the session. Explain that these are some more common prefixes and suffixes that students might come across when reading. When they are added to a word they change its meaning, for example:

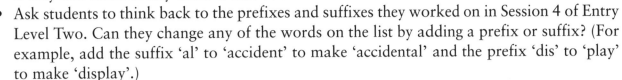

| friendly | + | un | = | unfriendly |
| (nice/like a friend) | | (prefix) | | (unwelcoming/unlike a friend) |

Alternatively they can transform one part of speech into another, for example:

| friend | + | ly | = | friendly |
| *(noun* – name given to a person you get on well with) | | (suffix) | | *(adjective* – means 'like a friend') |

- Give out copies of Activity Sheet 32, 'Changing words' and go through the information at the top of the sheet before asking students to have a go at completing the activities. You might like to start them off with the following examples: 'dress' + 'un' = 'undress' and 'hope' + 'less' = 'hopeless'.
- Discuss answers once everyone in the group has finished.

Activity 4 Focus exercise

- Students should work in pairs for this activity. Give out an assortment of newspaper and magazine articles to each pair. Ask them to highlight any words that have been changed by adding a prefix or suffix to a root word. They should then list these on a piece of paper. Try and spend some time with each pair as they are working through their activities. This will give you a chance to judge levels of understanding and to see if anyone is having problems getting to grips with the topic.
- Round off the activity with a group discussion. How did the students find the exercise? Enjoyable? Difficult? Encourage them to tell you why.
- As an extension to this activity ask students to look up the meaning of the root words they have just identified. Next tell them to look up the meaning of the word with its prefix or

suffix. Do they differ much? This exercise will give students an opportunity to do some valuable dictionary work. Once they have all finished, hold a short discussion to find out what students have discovered.

Activity 5   Explanation/idea storm

- Explain that when certain suffixes are added to root words the tense of the word is changed.
- Remind students about the work they did on tenses in Entry Level Two (Session 4). Write the following on the board: 'ed' = past tense and 'ing' = present tense. Use the word play to demonstrate past and present tense.
- Point out that when you want to change the tense of a sentence, you need to alter the verbs in the sentence by adding or removing suffixes. Ask the students to call out a few examples of verbs and write these on the board. Demonstrate how to change a couple into past and present tenses and then see if the students know how to change the word into the future tense (remind them that verbs can comprise more than one word). Explain that verbs can be changed to future tense by adding words such as 'will', 'is going to' and 'might'. For example, 'will play later' uses the verb 'play' in its future tense – 'will play'.

Ws/
E3.1, 2, 3
Ww/
E3.1, 2, 3
- Arrange students into twos and give each pair one of the sheets of flipchart that you prepared before the start of the session. Ask them to write some sentences using the verbs in their past, present and future tenses. The sentences should be complete and grammatically correct.
- End by taking feedback from the paired activity.

Activity 6   Explanation/focus exercise

Ww/
E3.1, 2
Rw/
E3.1, 3, 4
Tell the students that they are now going to do some more work on spelling. Remind the group that a good spelling strategy is to break words down into sounds (phonemes) and beats (syllables). (You might like to show them copies of Handout 27, 'Strategies to help improve your spelling' from p. 86, which you used in the previous level.) Ask the students to start by selecting eight words from their course words list.

When they have done so ask them to break four of the words into phonemes and four into syllables. They should then practise their dictionaries skills by looking up these words and writing their meanings in the dictionary section of their Workbooks (pp. 90–115).

As a further extension to this activity ask the students to arrange the words in alphabetical order. This is a perfect example of where an activity at a higher level can be used to reinforce one of the most basic elements of reading and writing.

Activity 7   Focus exercise

End the session with an 'Unfamiliar words' quiz. (Don't forget to stress the 'fun' aspect of the activity to your students!) Explain that you are going to call out some unfamiliar words and you want students to write them down as they think they ought to be spelt.

As soon as you have finished reading them out ask the students to tell you how they think the words should be spelt. Don't tell them whether they are right or wrong just yet. Instead, ask the students, individually, to check the spelling of each word in a dictionary.

Finish off by discussing how many they got right, what type of mistakes they made, and so on.

Specialist words

Below is a list of words and phrases that you will come across during your course.

accident	cognitive	breast-feeding
identity	centile-charts	surveillance
asthma	creative	development
reflexes	weaning	confidentiality
attachment	child-abuse	developmental
theories	social-development	cultural
viruses	allergies	bullying
separation-anxiety	play	child-protection

Try putting these into alphabetical order using first and second letters.

Rw/E3.5
Ww/E3.2

ACTIVITY SHEET 32

Changing words

Here are some more commonly used and seen prefixes and suffixes:

Prefixes – *dis, pre, un, de, re*

Suffixes – *ful, ly, less, ness,*

Examples of their use:

appear + dis = disappear   *wonder + ful = wonderful*
vent + pre = prevent   *playful + ly = playfully*
tidy + un = untidy   *soft + ness = softness*
light + de = delight   *use + less = useless*
fresh + re = refresh

ACTIVITIES

What prefixes can you add to the following words?

dress   play   write   sent

How many different words can you make out of 'hope' and 'help', just by adding suffixes? (Write your answers below)

hope   help

SESSION 2

Outline

In this session students will be building on skills they learnt in the last session and moving on to do some sentence work. As well as reinforcing what they already know about nouns, verbs and adjectives, students will be introduced to adverbs and the rules of grammar, and will have a chance to apply their knowledge as they construct texts of their own.

> For this session you will need:
>
> - A sheet of flipchart with the words *wanted, play, sent, bully, physical* and *help* written on it. Leave space underneath each one to write another word.
> - Enough unfamiliar words for a team quiz (teams are to have one word each).

Activities

Activity 1 Introduction

- Remind students about the prefix and suffix work they did in the last session. Do a brief recap using the words on the flipchart. They can be changed to *unwanted, display, present, bullying, physically* and *helpless*.
- Ask students to look up the meaning of any of the words they are unsure of. This is a good point to find out how students are getting on with dictionary work and using spelling strategies. Has anyone come across any new ones since you started to experiment with them in Entry Level Two?
- You might also like to discuss the use of the spellcheck program on a computer. First of all see if any of the students have ever used it and whether or not they found it helpful. Point out to students that while a spellcheck facility is useful it is of limited use until the user can judge or see how appropriate the changes are. Sometimes the changes suggested do not make sense in the context of what is being written. If students want to use it, they should do so for limited tasks only and ask someone to check any changes they are unsure of.

SLlr/
E3.1, 2,
3, 4, 5, 6
SLc/
E3.1, 2
SLd/
E3.2, 3

Activity 2 Explanation/focus exercise

- Explain to the students that the next few activities will be devoted to sentence work. Start off with a brief recap on nouns, verbs and sentence types.
- Remind the group that, as they know, verbs and nouns are parts of speech and we use them all the time. When we are writing they fill our sentences with lots of information. Explain that it is possible to make our sentences bigger and more interesting by adding information about the verbs and nouns. Show an example of what you mean on the board: write the words '*Today it is raining*' and ask students to identify the verb and the noun. Now write, '*Today is cold and it is raining heavily.*'
- Point out to students that you now have a better picture of what the day is like, and the sentence is longer and flows more smoothly. You have added a word about the verb 'raining' (*heavily*), called an ADVERB and a word describing the noun 'today' (*cold*), called an ADJECTIVE. (Remind students that they first looked at adjectives in Session 6 of

Entry Level Two. Can they remember the 'Adaptable adjectives' handout you gave them (Handout 32 on p. 104) and the sentences they wrote about something they enjoyed and something they did not (Activity Sheet 20 on p. 105)?)

- Give out copies of Handout 40, 'Adjectives and adverbs' and go through it with the students. Ask them to complete the activity at the bottom of the handout.

- Next ask students to complete the 'What can I add to these?' exercise on Activity Sheet 33. Discuss answers as a group once all the students have finished.

Activity 3   Discussion/focus exercise

- Explain to the students that when we write and build sentences we cannot do it by adding words randomly here and there. If we were to do this our writing would not make sense. Sentences have to be constructed according to the rules of GRAMMAR and PUNCTUATION.

Ws/ E3.1, 2, 3 SLlr/ E3.2, 3, 4, 5, 6

- Give out copies of Handout 41, 'Grammar' and discuss the various rules with the students. Ask them to complete the activity at the end of the handout. Collect feedback at the end of the exercise.

- Arrange students into pairs and ask them individually to compose three compound sentences – a question, an exclamation and a statement. They should make sure that their grammar and punctuation are correct. When everyone in the group has finished, ask them to swap their work over with a partner and to read out each other's sentences. Discuss the meaning of the sentences: do they make sense? Are they punctuated correctly and how did the punctuation affect reading? Which linking words have been used? Encourage listeners to show that they are paying attention and to ask questions if necessary.

Activity 4   Focus exercise

- Tell the students that having written some sentences they are now going to use them to build text.

- Give each student a copy of Activity Sheet 34, 'Text building' and go through the points one by one. Ask the students to write their text on a separate sheet of paper and to ensure that they consider each of the points listed on the activity sheet.

SLc/ E3.1, 3, 4 SLlr/ E3.1, 2, 3, 4, 5, 6

- When the students have finished the activity they should be encouraged to read their writing out to the rest of the group. (You might like to divide them into smaller groups or pairs for this exercise, depending on how students feel about talking in front of their classmates.) Listeners should check for general sense and meaning and should ask questions about what has been written. Stress how important it is for listeners to show they are paying attention by facial expression, eye contact, etc.

Activity 5   Focus exercise

End the session with a 'What's my meaning?' quiz. Put students into teams. Give each team one unfamiliar word from the list you made before the session started. Ask them to look up the true meaning of the word in a dictionary and write it down. They should then make up two definitions of their own and write them down with the true meaning. Once this has been done teams should take it in turns to read out the three meanings that they have written down and the other teams have to try and guess which is the correct meaning. The team that guesses the most correct meanings wins.

Adjectives and adverbs

When we are writing we need to give information about what we are writing about. The focus of what we write about is usually in the form of a noun or verb.

We use particular parts of speech to add information to verbs and nouns:

> ✳ We add information to verbs using ADVERBS
>
> ✳ We add information to nouns using ADJECTIVES

These are both words that begin with *ad* and their job is to *add* information to our writing.

Here are some examples of each:

ADJECTIVES	ADVERBS
big	quickly
small	soon
dangerous	very
new	happily

ACTIVITY

Try adding adjectives or adverbs to these sentences (write your answers alongside):

1. The dog ran down the road.
2. It was a place.
3. She had a dress on.
4. The children went outside.

142

What can I add to these?

Below are four brief, simple sentences. They do not give us much information!

What adjectives and adverbs can you add to them to give more information? (*As always, check for spelling, grammar, meaning and sense!*)

1. The children are playing.

2. The baby is crying.

3. Today it is sunny.

4. The children went for a walk.

Can you compose another simple sentence for each of the above, which could be joined to them to make compound sentences?

Grammar

Grammar is the rules of writing.

Why do we need rules?

We need to make our writing make sense to others.

What are these rules for?

They are the rules of language relating to how you combine words to make sentences and text.

Let's take a look at a couple:

✓ VERB TENSE

Verbs are words of action. The tense of the verb tells us at what time – past, present or future – the action takes place. The tense should be the same throughout the sentence.

✓ SUBJECT-VERB AGREEMENT

The subject is what a sentence is about. The subject 'governs' the verb. For example, if the subject is singular (one of) the verb must also be singular. If the subject is plural (more than one) the verb must also be plural. If there is more than one verb in the sentence, the subject rules them all.

Examples:

1. The **baby** *is happy* today. (singular **subject** = singular *verb*)
2. The **babies** *are happy* today. (plural **subject** = plural *verb*)
3. The **babies** *are happy* today and *are playing* in the water. (plural **subject** = plural *verbs*)

HANDOUT 41 continued

✓ WORD ORDER

The meaning of a sentence not only depends on the words we use but the order in which we use them. Most of the time we use words in the right order without thinking about it, but there are times when it is easy to make mistakes.

✳ Words in the wrong place

The nursery nurse picked up the child who had fallen over quickly.

This sounds like the child had fallen over quickly. Not so! Try this:

The nursery nurse quickly picked up the child who had fallen over.

Sounds better, doesn't it?

✳ Group of words in the wrong place

The student heard the children using the musical instruments who were singing.

Sounds like the musical instruments were singing, doesn't it? I don't think so! Try it like this:

The student heard the children, who were singing, using the musical instruments.

Sounds more like it!

ACTIVITY

Have a go at sorting these sentences out (you can write your answers below each one):

1. The children saw the bees walking round the playground.

2. I saw a little girl with her mother who was arguing.

3. Children by the age of five years can become self-confident.

4. The child were very sick after swallowing the paint.

5. The children is very noisy.

6. Children at the age of two is able to say fifty words.

Text building

Choose a sentence from the three you have just composed. Your task is to write a text of two paragraphs, built around the sentence.

You should make sure that:

✓ You use the correct punctuation

✓ You have subject–verb agreement

✓ The tense is correct throughout

✓ You have used a verb in every sentence

✓ You have used a mixture of compound and simple sentences

✓ You have checked your spelling

✓ You have checked the text to see that it makes sense

SESSION 3

Outline

The object of this session is to build on the word and sentence work done in Session 2 and to explore a larger range of texts, looking at punctuation marks in particular.

For this session you will need:

- Three examples of instructional texts, e.g. fire evacuation procedures, how to use a photocopier, etc. You will need one copy per student.
- A selection of short texts that are more than one paragraph in length, e.g. newspaper article, holiday brochure, fiction, advertisements, etc.
- Copies of an assortment of letters written for different purposes, e.g. informal 'thank you' letters, official business letters, letters home to parents, etc.
- Different coloured highlighter pens.

Activities

Activity 1 Introduction

- Start by explaining to learners that when we read text we see it written down in a variety of ways. As childcare students they will come across many different texts, some of which will be written for the purposes of 'instruction'.
- Have an idea storming session to generate thoughts about when students might need to read instructions during their training. Suggestions might include:

  - while making babies' feeds
  - using equipment
  - fire and evacuation procedures
  - putting equipment together
  - homework or assignments
  - activity sheets
  - activities for children to do
  - recipes
  - when using the Internet
  - getting to placement
  - filling in forms.

 • Recap the characteristics of instructional text: a series of steps that takes the reader through a process, from start to finish, until it is complete. Give out copies of Handout 42, 'How to make a shaker' as an example and go through it with the students.

 • Give out copies of Activity Sheet 35, 'Instruction or statement?' and ask students to complete the exercise. Discuss answers once everyone has finished.

Activity 2   Group discussion/focus exercise

Rt/E3.3
Rs/E3.3

Give out the three examples of instructional texts that you prepared before the start of the session. Discuss the common features of the texts: all three begin with an opening statement revealing the purpose of the activity; the set of instructions is broken down into individual sentences/steps; the reader is addressed directly and told exactly what to do.

Point out that the texts use verbs in order to describe the exact actions that a reader is required to take. You should also explain that instructions can be set out in a variety of ways: bullet points, arrows, numbered lists, etc.

Ask students to write out a set of instructions, e.g. for making a cup of tea or putting on a nappy. When they have written them out, ask the students to put the same instructions into different formats. End the activity by discussing the different formats people have used. Tell students to keep their sets of instructions safe as they'll be using them again at the end of Session 6.

Wt/E3.3
Rt/E3.3

Activity 3   Discussion/focus exercise

Recap different text types covered in Session 8 of Entry Level Two. Remind students that texts are written in a format and style that suits the writer's purpose. However, some texts of the same type may have different purposes. Letters are one such example and have a particular way of being set out.

Give out copies of Handout 43, 'Letters' and identify the purpose and language of each one, discussing the following points as a group:

Rt/E3.2

- Letter 1 is a business letter; the language is formal and the letter ends and is signed formally.
- Letter 2 is to a friend; the language is informal and chatty, and the writer has signed off informally.
- Letter 3 is a circular letter sent to parents and is not addressed to any one person in particular; the language is formal but not to the same extent as the business letter. It is not signed but has the name and designation of the person it is from.

Look at and discuss the selection of letters you have brought in. See if students can differentiate between those written for business purposes and those for pleasure. Can they identify which letters are personal and which are official? Discuss the use of formal and informal language with the group. What sort of responses do each of the different letter types generate?

Rt/
E3.1, 2
SLd/
E3.1, 2, 3

Activity 4   Focus exercise

Rt/
E3.1, 2
SLd/
E3.1, 2, 3

- Students should work together in small groups for this activity. Give each group a selection of texts that you gathered before the start of the session and ask them to discuss the following:

  – What is it about?
  – Where could it have come from?
  – How can you tell?
  – How can you tell what it is about?

SLlr/
E3.3, 5, 6
SLc/
E3.1, 3, 4
SLd/
E3.1, 2, 3
  – What do the first lines tell you and is it a good introduction to the text/article?
  – Do the endings sum up the article/text or do they finish it off?
  – How does the text end?

- Once they have dealt with these questions, each group should take it in turns to tell the rest of the class about their texts. Encourage the other students to ask questions.

Rt/3.1, 2
- After the presentations, point out that the beginning and end of sentences in a text can give valuable clues as to what it is about. The type of language used, the students' understanding of grammar and punctuation, and the ability to decode words will all play a part in helping learners to work out, predict and check the meaning of a text.

- Give each student a copy of Activity Sheet 36, 'Finish 'em off' and ask them to complete the exercise.

- Discuss the group's choice of endings: why one ending as opposed to another? What clues did they get from the text, e.g. common words, titles, etc.?

Activity 5   Explanation/focus exercise

- Tell students that another element that helps us to understand text is PUNCTUATION. Remind students that they covered basic forms of punctuation at the end of Entry Level Two. Recap question marks, exclamation marks and full stops and what they signify in written text.

- Explain that you are now going to look at some new kinds of punctuation marks. Distribute copies of Handout 44, 'More punctuation' around the class and go through it with the students.

Rs/E3.3
- Once you are confident that students are happy with this, give them copies of Activity Sheet 37, 'Child observation' and ask them to read it and identify commas and speech marks.

Activity 6   Focus exercise

Rs/E3.3
Use the texts from Activity 4 in this activity. Ask students to read the texts again and identify any punctuation marks they recognise, listing the different sorts on a sheet of paper.

Discuss the various kinds of punctuation marks and what they have been used for. How does it help us to understand the text?

Ws/E3.1
Activity 7   Focus exercise

End the session by asking students to pick a text from the ones they have been working on during the session and to write a few notes to summarise it briefly. Remind them that as they write they should be thinking about all the topics that have been covered in this session.

How to make a shaker

You will need:

☐ A plastic bottle with a screw-on top
☐ Dried pasta, peas or rice
☐ Non-toxic paint
☐ Strong non-toxic glue
☐ Decorative bits and pieces

FIRST wash the bottle thoroughly inside and outside and remove any labels. Make sure it is thoroughly dry inside and out.

NEXT put the dried peas/pasta etc. in the bottle – make sure you leave enough room in the bottle for it to move around and make a noise when shaken. Seal the bottle securely.

THEN paint the container with non-toxic paint. When dry, decorate with colourful bits and pieces, stuck on with the strong non-toxic glue.

LASTLY allow it to dry.

You will have an inexpensive, colourful musical instrument suitable for a toddler or young child.

ACTIVITY SHEET 35

Instruction or statement?

Look at the phrases below and decide whether they are instructions or statements (write your answers alongside):

Meet me at 10 a.m.

Come to the staffroom.

We'll see you there.

Change the baby's nappy in the bathroom.

Write in BLOCK CAPITALS.

Sign here.

Way out.

This way up.

Fire Exit.

Paint cupboard.

Letters

Here is a selection of letters written for different purposes and containing different sorts of information and language.

Letter 1

Happy Store
New Road
Birmingham
B22 4PY

Mr Jones
Old Road
Birmingham
B22 5BW

Dear Mr Jones,

Thank you for your letter of the 31/1/02 in which you outlined your complaint about events of 30/1/02, which took place at this store.

I am writing to inform you that a full investigation into the matter has taken place. The member of staff, named in your letter, has admitted she was very rude to you.

On behalf of the company I would like you to accept our apologies and assure you that appropriate action has been taken.

Please accept this voucher for £25, which can be spent in any of our stores, by way of compensation for your experience.

Yours sincerely,

U.N.O. Who

U.N.O. Who
Director of Public Relations

Letter 2

Hi Raj,

How are you? I hope you are well!

It was so great to see you last week. What a surprise! I couldn't believe my eyes when I saw you coming towards me.

Since I bumped into you, I decided to get in touch with some of the others from our old 'gang'.

Tal and Ros are doing a childcare course and Sobia is training to be a teacher. Imagine that, Sobia a teacher – she hated school!

Anyway, when we got chatting we thought it would be nice to have a get-together – are you up for it? How about Friday 22nd at 8 p.m., my flat? You can stay the night if you want.

It would be so much fun – PLEEEASE COME!

Let me know soon,

Luv you

Bushra

Letter 3

Primary School
Lake Street

1st June 2003

Dear parents,

SUMMER FAIR

It's that time of year again. Time to be thinking about holding our annual summer fair.

The date has been set for 27th June, 1 p.m. until 4 p.m., on the school playing fields.

We already have some ideas for stalls and entertainment but we need more!

If you would like to book a stall or have any ideas for stalls or entertainment please contact the school secretary as soon as possible.

The staff and pupils at the school appreciate your continued support at these events.

We look forward to seeing you there, so please make a note in your diary.

M. Smith

Mary Smith
(Headteacher)

ACTIVITY SHEET 36

Finish 'em off!

Below are three pieces of writing without their endings. There is a selection of endings on the second page of the activity sheet. Which ending would you finish off each piece of writing with and why?

---

(1) WEANING

Weaning is the process of getting babies to take solid foods. By the age of six months, milk alone is not enough for them. They need a wider variety of foods for:

- getting all the nutrients they need
- meeting the baby's needs for more food
- learning to chew
- family socialisation at mealtimes

When making the decision about when to start weaning, it is best to be guided by your baby. Good signs that your baby is ready to be weaned are:

---

(2) INTEREST TABLES

Interest tables are excellent for displaying things that are of particular interest to children. They can be used for themes, festivals, displays and many more topics. They are a very good way of giving children a chance to handle unfamiliar objects and a great way to stimulate conversation.

---

(3) A BALANCED DIET

To grow and develop, children need a diet that contains the different essential nutrients. These nutrients are needed for children to stay healthy, grow and develop. The essential nutrients are:

- carbohydrate
- fat
- protein
- vitamins
- minerals
- and, last but by no means least, fluids

© June Green (2003) *Basic Skills for Childcare – Literacy*. Published by David Fulton Publishers Ltd.

Endings

Below are four text endings. Three of them are for the texts on the first page of this activity sheet. Which ending goes with which text? What could the remaining ending be from?

Ending 1

These nutrients are gained from eating a range of different foods.

Ending 2

Children, parents and staff can be encouraged to bring in items of interest. For example, a special toy, an object from home and different cultural artefacts.

Ending 3

To destroy bacteria on food, foods should be heated to a temperature of 72°C for several minutes.

Ending 4

- baby seems hungry
- baby wakes up hungry in the night
- baby doesn't gain weight as she/he should
- baby is restless and cries a lot

HANDOUT 44

More punctuation

Speech marks

- These are also sometimes known as *inverted commas.*
- They mark off what someone is saying from the rest of the text.
- There will be two at the beginning of what the speaker is saying and two at the end. For example: the teacher said "Let's settle down for story-time", and the children sat down quietly on their cushions.

Commas

These are marks that are found within text sentences. They have a few functions, the main ones of which are:

- to separate or break up parts of a sentence.
- to separate words in a list.

For example:

1. In some cases it doesn't take long for the baby to learn how to get food from spoon to mouth, but it can get very messy.
2. You will need paper, glue, scissors and old magazines.

ACTIVITY SHEET 37

Child observation

Have a look at the text below and see if you can spot the speech marks and commas. Highlight them in a different colour.

Child A is 3.2 years old, has been at nursery for six months and has two older sisters. I am observing child A playing a board game with three other children.

There is a childcare worker supervising the children. Child A throws the dice. "It's a four", she says and moves her counter four spaces. She then hands the dice to child B. Child A waits patiently while children B, C and D take their turns. It is now her turn again – she picks up the dice and throws it on the table. "Three", she says. She moves her counter three spaces.

The childcare worker points out to A that she has landed on a space that says she must miss her next turn. Child A looks a bit upset but does not say anything. She hands the dice to child B. Child D shouts "I want a go, give it to me". Child A moves to stand by child D and tells him "It's not your turn, you are after C". D shouts "NO" to child A. She moves back to her chair saying, " You must wait until it is your go". The childcare worker intervenes and the game continues. Child A waits patiently until her turn comes round and claps excitedly when she gets a high number. When the game is finished, child A and child C help the childcare worker to put the game away.

Outline

The focus of this session is reading text and the variety of approaches we might take, i.e. skimming, scanning and detailed reading. As well as developing these skills students will be identifying main points and ideas within texts and looking at different layouts.

> For this session you will need:
>
> • A variety of TV magazines or listings pages from newspapers.
> • Some articles cut out from a variety of newspapers.

Activities

Activity 1 Introduction

• First, explain to students that we all need a reason to read otherwise the process gets boring and has no point.

• Hold a discussion around the following question: why do we read? Suggestions might include the following: for entertainment purposes, to get information, studying, instructions and directions.

Rt/E3.6 • Point out that we do not have to read every single word of a text. Some students may be surprised to hear this! Give out copies of Handout 45, 'Reading' and go through the various techniques with the students.

Activity 2 Focus exercise

To clarify the information given in the handout, give out the articles from magazines and newspapers, which you prepared before the start of the session. Give students 30 seconds to look at the article and to write down what it is about and how they can tell. Take feedback from the group once the time is up.

As a further extension to this exercise, arrange students in pairs and give out the TV magazines and listings pages from newspapers. Tell students to go through them as if they were skimming to find something in particular, e.g. a film time. Encourage them to refer back to the techniques described in Handout 45 if they get stuck. Once the group has finished, discuss findings and ask students to comment on how the bits of information stood out. Point out that students have been using the skimming technique.

Activity 3 Focus exercise

• Students should stay in their pairs for this activity. Using the same TV listings as above, allocate some specific days and times to each pair and ask them to find the titles of films that appear at those particular dates and times. Explain that they should use the scanning technique to do this.

• At the end of the exercise discuss how effective the group felt the scanning technique was. What led them to the information they were asked to find?

- Students should now swap magazine/newspaper pages with another pair while you give out copies of Activity Sheet 38, 'When is it on?' Ask them to read through the questions on the sheet and to have a go at answering them one by one. As they do so they should write notes on a separate piece of paper briefly explaining how they used the skimming and scanning techniques during the exercise.
- Once everyone has finished discuss how it went. How did the students find information? What helped them to find it?

Activity 4   Discussion/focus exercise

- Explain that images are often included within text and can give meaning and information to the reader. Discuss the type of images that may be seen in text. You might like to start the group off with a few suggestions, e.g. maps, diagrams, photographs, pictures, symbols, etc.
- End the session with the 'What goes where?' activity on Activity Sheet 39. Students can work in pairs or individually for this.
- Discuss answers when everyone has finished. Who got the most right?

HANDOUT 45

Reading

When we read we do it for a reason. If we didn't we would get bored very quickly.

Some reasons for reading:

✳ Entertainment, e.g. magazines, newspapers, books, jokes and cartoon strips.

✳ Information, e.g. finding a phone number, looking for the time of a TV programme or finding out when a film is on at the cinema.

✳ Studying, e.g. for an assignment, for an exam or just to know more!

✳ Instructions/directions, e.g. how to get somewhere, how to make something or what to do for an assignment.

When we read we do not need to read every word. There are three techniques we can use depending on our need:

1 SKIMMING

This when we skim some text to get a general idea of what the text is about or to find out whether it is useful. Think of a stone skimming across water – it just touches the surface. It's the same when you skim in reading.

2 SCANNING

When you look for a specific piece of information within some text. You've skimmed and think it might be useful, now you are looking a bit more carefully. That stone is now bouncing across the water, dipping in here and there.

3 DETAILED READING

This is when you read the text carefully to understand it or to take notes for your work. The stone likes the feel of the water and has sunk into it!

Using these techniques can save you valuable time and unnecessary work, especially when doing assignments.

Things that give you clues when skimming and scanning:

SKIMMING	SCANNING
Titles	Keywords related to the topic
Headings	Use of italics, bold print and underlining
Subheadings	
Indexes	Dates and times in TV magazines
Illustrations	Bullet points
Images	Numbered points
Words at the top of	Order and format of the writing
a page, e.g. in a	Relevance, e.g. language and
dictionary or	words used
phone directory	

Rt/
E3.6, 7, 8

ACTIVITY SHEET 38

When is it on?

You have had a bit of practice at finding information in TV magazines and TV pages. Now we want you to look at the listings in a little more detail. As you do the activity below, make notes on how you are using the skimming and scanning techniques to help you.

Find out the following from the TV magazine you have been given. (Write your answers beneath each question)

1. What time is the news on BBC after 7pm, on a weekday night?

2. How long is the news on for?

3. Which terrestrial channels have children's TV on them?

4. Is children's TV on at the same time every day on these channels?

5. What time does children's TV start and finish on these channels?

6. Pick one day and list the children's TV programmes that are shown on each channel on that day.

What goes where?

Match the topics to their images.

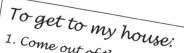

To get to my house:
1. Come out of the school gates and turn right.
2. Go straight ahead at the crossroads, and then turn right, opposite the park gates.
3. Mine is the third house on the left.

PISCES ★ ★ ★ ★
As Jupiter moves into the part of your chart relating to money, it's time to watch your dosh!
★ ★ ★ ★

DAY 3
On the third day of your city break, you'll tour around the key sights of Paris, climbing to the top of its most famous landmark.

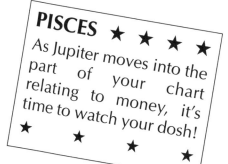

It will be a blustery day with a mixture of sunny spells and scattered showers.

SESSION 5

Outline

In this session students will be reinforcing the reading skills developed in the previous session but in a context that relates directly to their course. The activities in this session are based around researching for a childcare assignment. It is important that students realise that the skills they are developing are not confined to Basic Skills sessions but are transferable and apply to everything they do.

> For this session you will need:
>
> • Current newspapers
> • Highlighter pens
> • Yellow Pages
> • Telephone directory
> • Local A–Z
> • Childcare textbooks.

Activities

Activity 1 Introduction

Recap skimming/scanning and detailed reading by giving out newspapers, putting a list of current topics on the board and asking students to use their skim/scan techniques to find them in the newspaper. You could make this more fun by timing the activity and seeing who finds the most in the time allocated.

Rw/E3.4 ### Activity 2 Explanation

- Explain that when reading text there are some parts of what we read that are more important to the meaning of the text than others. Give students the following example: If you were reading to find out which physical skills a baby develops in the first year of life, one of the following texts would be more meaningful to you than the other:

  (a) *Different skill types*
  (b) *Ages and stages of development*

  Can they tell you which it is?

Rt/E3.5 - Give out copies of Handout 46, 'Physical development' and the highlighter pens. (Students might like to staple the sheets of the handout together so pages don't get lost.) Explain to students that this four-page handout is about the development of physical skills and how to promote them in the first year of life. Ask them to highlight the parts that would be most meaningful to them if they were doing an activity to list the skills developed at certain ages.

- Once the students have worked through the handout discuss what they have highlighted and why.

- Remind students that context is a useful clue when trying to work something out. For example, this handout is about an area of children's development so there are likely to be lots of words students already know, e.g. 'development', 'child' and so on. There may also be some parts of words that students recognise, e.g. 'child' within 'children' or 'development' within 'developmental'. Remind students to use this technique plus their own knowledge of words to help them decipher unfamiliar ones.

- Ask students to read through the handout again and to make a list of any unfamiliar words they come across. Spend some time working on strategies to remember these words. This can be done in pairs/small groups or as a whole-class activity.

Activity 3 Group discussion/focus exercise

We now want the students to try locating some information for themselves. Hold a short discussion based on the following question: Where do you look when you want to find something out? You might like to start the group off with a few suggestions, e.g. contents pages, index, directories, A–Z, information leaflets, posters, etc.

Divide the students into small groups and give out the Yellow Pages, telephone directory and the local A–Z. Distribute copies of Activity Sheet 40, 'Where is it and how do I get there?' around the class and ask students to complete the exercise. Point out that they will need to bring this work with them to Session 7 of Entry Level Three.

As a follow-on from this exercise, hand out a selection of childcare textbooks and ask students to find information on:

- Social development
- Behavioural development
- Albert Bandura
- B. F. Skinner.

Students should make a list of:

- The book title
- The chapter or section
- Page numbers
- Where they found the information (you will need to photocopy these so they can be used again in Session 7).

Activity 4 Reflection

End the session with a discussion about the different sources they have used today:

- Textbooks
- Handouts
- Local A–Z
- Telephone directory.

They will have used indexes, headings, contents pages, maps, lists, etc. to locate the information they wanted. Discuss the following points with the group:

- Layout
- Amount of detail
- Images
- Paragraph structure
- Which was the easiest to use and which was the hardest?
- Why?

Physical development

✳ By 'physical growth' we mean the rate at which our bodies grow when we are children. This includes weight and height.

✳ By 'physical development' we mean the gaining of skills that allow us to gain mobility and independence.

The skills gained in physical development can be divided into two main categories:

  1. Gross motor skills
  2. Fine manipulative skills

✳ *Gross motors skills* are the skills we use to move around, kick, throw, ride a bike, etc. We use our large muscles for these skills.

✳ *Fine manipulative skills* are the finer skills such as feeding ourselves, doing up buttons, tying shoelaces, etc. We use our smaller muscles for these skills.

When a baby is born the muscles are weak and have to grow and develop. The baby also has to learn how to use them. All this takes time but much of this development takes place in the first year of life.

NEWBORN BABY

The newborn baby has no control over his undeveloped muscles:

- When you pick a newborn baby up, his head will fall backwards.
- When the baby is held in a sitting position, his spine will curl up and the head will fall forwards
- A baby is born with a set of reflexes that help the baby to feed and survive.

THREE MONTHS OLD

- By this age the baby will be beginning to control his head. His back is much straighter but he will still need supporting when in a sitting position.
- When lying on his stomach, the baby's legs will be straighter instead of curved underneath him.
- Legs are strong enough to take a little weight when the baby is held in an upright position, but will still sag at the knees.
- Hands are open most of the time now and if given something to grasp, the baby will hold it for only a few seconds. The grasp reflex has gone.
- By four months, the baby will clasp his hands together and spend a lot of time looking at and playing with his fingers.
- When lying on his stomach, the baby is able to lift his head and shoulders from the floor and support them with his forearms.

SIX MONTHS OLD

- By this age the baby will have developed complete head control and is able to raise his head when lying on his back.
- He can sit unsupported for a little while if his hands are forward for support.
- His back is much stronger and he can sit on his own with some support at his back.
- During this stage the baby will learn to roll from front to back and then from back to front.
- He is able to take his weight on his legs and bounces up and down enthusiastically.
- He can lift his head and chest from the ground using straight arms to do so.

NINE MONTHS OLD

This is a stage of great physical development:

- The baby can pull into a sitting position and sit unsupported for a short while.
- He is able to move around the floor by rolling or pushing and pulling with hands.
- He can pull self into a standing position.
- He may start to walk sideways, using furniture for support or with both hands held by an adult.
- The baby is able to use fingers and thumb to hold an object.
- He opens hands to deliberately drop things.
- During this stage he will also develop the skill of pointing at objects and pushing them with his finger.
- By the age of ten months, the baby will be able to pick things up with the tip of his index finger and thumb.

ONE YEAR OLD

- The baby can now sit unsupported for a long while.
- He is able to turn sideways and stretch to pick something up.
- He can either crawl, 'bear-walk' or 'bottom-shuffle' to get around.
- The baby can walk with someone holding one of his hands. Feet appear to be going in different directions and steps are uncoordinated
- He is able to throw things.
- He points with his index finger to something he wants.
- Some babies will be walking by this age. If this is the case they have usually missed out the crawling stage or gone from crawling to walking very rapidly.

As you can see a lot of skills are gained in this first year of life. From here on in, young children will be building and fine-tuning these skills until they are able to move around independently, feed, dress, wash themselves, and so on.

Rt/E3.8
Wt/E3.3

ACTIVITY SHEET 40

Where is it and how do I get there?

You have just moved to the area. You are looking for a day nursery for your three-year-old son and a primary school for your six-year-old daughter. Follow the steps below.

1. In the Yellow Pages find one of each that is close to home or college.

2. Write down the name, address and telephone number of each setting.

3. Now find where they are in the local A–Z and work out how to get there from college or home.

4. Write the instructions out using bullet points or numbered instructions.

NOTE: You will need to bring this work with you to Session 7.

SESSION 6

Outline

The aim of this session is for students to think about the different sorts of texts they have looked at in the last few sessions and to develop a series of writing skills involved in the planning, construction and checking of text. As well as being introduced to some other text types and formats, by the end of the session students will have produced their own piece of text, from the early preparation of notes right through to the final proof-reading stage.

For this session you will need:

- Pupils' sets of instructions written in the Session 3 (Activity 2). Remind students to bring these with them to the session.

Activities

Activity 1   Introduction

- Recap texts that were explored in the last session. Explain to students that by the end of this session they will have planned, drafted and proof-read their own piece of text.
- Hold a group discussion based on the following question: What type of writing do we need to plan for? Assignments, essays and formal letters all fit into this category. Explain to the group that not all our writing needs to be planned, however. Sometimes we do it off the top of our heads.
- Invite students to write a list of either shopping they need to buy or things they have to do tomorrow.
- When they have finished point out that this piece of writing came straight from their heads. It didn't need structuring as it's simply a list to be used by them when they need it. It is merely a personal reminder and as long as they can understand it, that's OK. It isn't going to be read by anyone else.
- Can the learners think of any other texts that would not require any planning? Give them a few examples to start them off, e.g. text messages, emails, notes, reminders, messages in greeting cards, etc.

Activity 2   Explanation/focus exercise

The way you write something and the context in which you write it depends on who or what it is for.

- Give out copies of Handout 47, 'Purpose of writing' and go through it with the students. The group should then complete the activity on the sheet individually or in pairs.
- Explain that some pieces of writing will be done on pre-prepared formats, e.g. cheques, telephone message pads, accident books, child records, forms, and so on.
- Two of the pre-prepared formats that students are likely to use during their course are assignment submission forms and front sheets for child observations.
- Give out copies of Handout 48, 'Different formats' and discuss what sort of responses students think each format would require, e.g. formal, detailed, casual, etc., and why.

Activity 3 **Explanation/focus exercise**

- Explain to students that completing a form is fairly easy as you are usually answering questions or filling in boxes. Most of it will come straight from your head onto the paper. With free writing the process is not so easy. For example, a letter of complaint or an essay for your coursework will almost certainly take a bit more thought. Writers need to consider the following:

  - What to write
  - How to format it
  - How much detail to include
  - Whether to use formal or informal language
  - How to make sure it makes sense.

- Stress that it is worth taking time to do all this: the end product will be much improved, as writers they will feel good about what they have written and people will take notice of the writing since it has obviously taken great effort to produce.
- Give out copies of Activity Sheet 41, 'Planning writing' and ask students to complete the exercise.
- When the group have finished this explain that once you have planned what to include, the next step is to plan what goes where – the structure of the piece of writing.
- Give out copies of Handout 49, 'What goes where?' and go through it with the students. They need to have the notes under headings in front of them, which they prepared during the 'Planning writing' activity. Following the writing frame on Handout 49, ask them to put the notes into order and to arrange them in paragraphs.

Activity 4 **Focus exercise**

- Once students have finished planning they should have a go writing the first draft of their letter. Make sure they have an adequate amount of time in which to do this. Next arrange students in pairs and ask them to give the first draft of their letter to their partner to read. Point out that, while reading, students should be asking themselves the following questions:

  - Does it make sense?
  - Is there subject–verb agreement?
  - Is it written in correct tense throughout?
  - Are there any spelling mistakes?

- Explain to students that they are proof-reading or, in other words, checking the text for errors. Tell them that they will be looking at proof-reading in more detail in the next session.
- Students should then feed back views, concerns, etc. to their partner and suggest changes that might be made to the text. This is an important stage in the drafting process, so make sure that all students take on the role of both writer and reviewer.
- Once everyone has received feedback on their first attempt, give the group time to complete the final draft. Students should hand this in for marking.

Activity 5 Focus exercise

Students will need the set of instructions that they wrote in Session 3 (Activity 2) for this activity. Ask students to write out their instructions as a piece of continuous text. Remind students that instructional text needs to be written in a logical order. Recap chronological words, e.g. *first, next, then, lastly,* and instructional text from previous sessions/level.

End the session with students reading out their directions/instructions to their partner who then has to repeat them back to the reader WITHOUT LOOKING AT THEM!

HANDOUT 47

Purpose of writing

When we write we are influenced by the reason we are writing and who we are writing it for. This will influence:

Content   how much detail/amount of information should we give?

Format   list, paragraphs, notes or points?

Style   formal, informal or chatty?

Accuracy   should we use correct spelling and grammar or is slang OK?

ACTIVITY

What type of content, format, style and accuracy would be needed for the texts below?

Shopping list

Essay for your course   Business letter

Directions to your place, for a party!

Text message   Class activity   Work for a display

Course assignment – I have to pass this!

HANDOUT 48

Different formats

1

CERTIFICATE IN CHILDCARE
Assignment Submission Sheet

NAME: ....

PIN: ....

SUBMISSION DATE: ....

COMMENTS ON ASSIGNMENT: ....

....

SIGNATURE: ....

DATE: ....

2

Telephone message pad

Message for: ....

Date: ....

Time message taken: ....

Message: ....

Call back required: ....

Message taken by: ....

H A N D O U T 4 8 c o n t i n u e d

3

ASSIGNMENT CRITERIA TRACKING SHEET

ASSIGNMENT CRITERIA	PAGE	STUDENT	MARKER
Assignment task has been completed			
Identify stages of physical development from 2–4 years			
List physical care needs of children aged 2, 3 and 4 years			
Describe how four of these needs are met in the childcare setting			
Describe the role of the childcare worker in promoting the physical development of children age 2–4 years			
Describe one activity that will promote fine manipulative skills for children age 2, 3 and 4 years			
Describe one activity that will promote gross motor skills for children age 2, 3 and 4 years			
Identify how each activity will develop these skills			
Include references and bibliography			

4

Trainwell Training College

Thank you for showing interest in a course at this college. Please fill in the details below so that we can send you further information and dates of open days.

Name: ....

Address: ....

Telephone number: ....

Course(s) interested in: ....

Planning writing

When planning writing, for example for an essay or writing a formal letter, there are various things to consider:

- Who am I writing for?
- What am I writing about?
- What do I need to include?
- How much detail should I include?
- How should I organise my writing so that it makes sense?

The most important thing you need to plan is the CONTENT – what to include.

There are a few ways you do this:

✓ Lists
✓ Notes under headings
✓ Spidergrams
✓ Mind maps

Taking two of the formats above, page 2 of this activity sheet shows how you would use them to make notes in preparation for writing a letter of complaint about the poor service in a restaurant.

List format

What do I need to include?

* Date and time I was at the restaurant – meal booked for 7.30 p.m. on 18/12/02.
* First thing that went wrong – table not big enough for the size of our party, had booked for a party of 12.
* Attitude of staff when this was pointed out – grudgingly moved us to a bigger table.
* Length of time before they took our order – 15 minutes from time of being seated.
* Meals took ages to come – 20 minutes from ordering, when they did come two were wrong.
* When the bill came it was wrong – we were told it was a service charge – we refused to pay it as the service had been so poor.
* What do we want done about it – a 50% refund from the bill.

Spidergram format

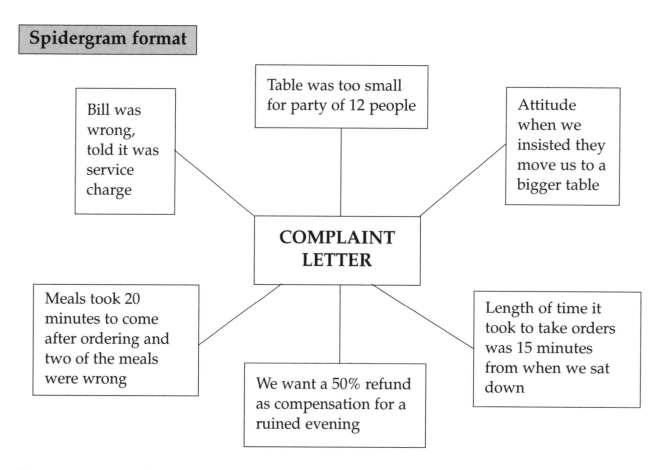

Try putting the above notes into the other two types of format mentioned. Can you think of any other ways to format the notes?

What goes where?

✓ You've planned what to include (spidergram, list, etc.)
✓ You've thought about the format
✓ You've thought about the style

Now you need to think about the structure.

Using the notes you have just been working on in Activity Sheet 41, plan the structure of your letter of complaint. Use the writing frame below as a guide. Remember that it needs to be written in the order the events happened.

Paragraph 1 – introduction
When/where/why/how?

Paragraph 2
Arrival, table too small, attitude of staff, etc.

Paragraph 3

Paragraph 4

Paragraph 5 – conclusion
Opinion, what you want to happen.

Now you have planned your letter, you are ready to write the first draft.

© June Green (2003) *Basic Skills for Childcare – Literacy*. Published by David Fulton Publishers Ltd.

SESSION 7

Outline

The focus of this final session of Entry Level Three is on reading and writing text. Students will start by exploring some more texts, looking more closely at paragraphs and proof-reading introduced previously. The session will culminate in students writing their own pieces of text. This activity will not only reinforce previous skills while developing new ones, it will also engender an enormous sense of achievement in the learners.

For this session you will need:

- A selection of photocopied texts, each one at least three paragraphs long.

- The photocopied text from the childcare books used in Session 5 (Activity 3).

Activities

Activity 1 Introduction

- Explain to students that they are going to begin by looking at and comparing two pieces of text. Give out copies of Handout 50 and ask the group to have a quick glance at Text 1. Discuss first impressions with the students. What strikes them about this text?
- Would they choose to read the whole thing? Why or why not?
- Now ask them to glance at Text 2 and discuss it in the same way as you did for Text 1.
- Compare the two pieces: while each contains the same wording, Text 1 is continuous whereas Text 2 is broken into paragraphs. Which would students find easier to read and why?
- Explain to the group that continuous text often looks daunting and can be off-putting to a reader. Alternatively text which is arranged into paragraphs looks easier to read and breaking text down into chunks makes it easier to manage. Paragraphs give text structure and meaning.

Rt/E3.1 ### Activity 2 Focus exercise

Give out copies of Handout 51, 'Paragraphs' and go through each point with the group. Follow this up by distributing the photocopied texts of three or more paragraphs, which you collected before the session started. Ask the students to:

1. Identify the main points and ideas in each paragraph.

2. Explain what the topic sentence tells us.

Activity 3 Explanation/focus exercise

- Remind students about the third activity of Session 5 where they had to look for some information in childcare textbooks.
- Give students the photocopied text from Session 5 and copies of Handout 52, 'The task' explaining what they will be doing for the remainder of the session.

- Make sure students have access to the 'Planning writing' activity sheet from Session 6 (Activity Sheet 41) and the 'Paragraphs' handout they looked at in the previous activity. In addition to these, each student should be given a copy of Handout 53, 'Editing your first draft' and Handout 54, 'Proof-reading'. Go through both of these with the group.
- For a bit of extra support a planning sheet has been provided for them in Handout 55, which will give the students a few reminders of strategies they looked at in previous sessions.
- Spend the rest of this session and any further time needed to complete this task. The activity will bring together many of the word, sentence and text level skills that students have been developing for both reading and writing.

This task marks the end of Entry Level Three. Lots of constructive and positive feedback should be given for each piece of work. For many students, writing their own piece of text is a mammoth task and an enormous achievement. It should be recognised and celebrated as such.

HANDOUT 50

TEXT 1

If you want to work with young children you need to be a qualified nursery nurse. To get a qualification you need to go to college. To get a diploma in childcare you have to do a two-year course. Some of the time you will be at placement and some of the time at college. At college you will learn all the theory about children. You will learn about how they grow and develop, what they need to grow and develop, how they learn, food they need, how to keep them safe, activities to do with them and how to get a job. You will also learn about health promotion and caring for sick children. There are assignments to do and you have to complete some child observations. At placement you put into practice what you learn at college. It is very hard work but very enjoyable too.

TEXT 2

If you want to work with young children you need to be a qualified nursery nurse. To get a qualification you need to go to college.

To get a diploma in childcare you have to do a two-year course. Some of the time you will be at placement and some of the time at college.

At college you will learn all the theory about children. You will learn about how they grow and develop, what they need to grow and develop, how they learn, food they need, how to keep them safe, activities to do with them and how to get a job. You will also learn about health promotion and caring for sick children.

There are assignments to do and you have to complete some child observations.

At placement you put into practice what you learn at college. It is very hard work but very enjoyable too.

Paragraphs

❑ Paragraphs are units of writing.

❑ A paragraph is usually made up of more than one sentence.

❑ Each paragraph is based on its own topic or idea.

❑ Paragraphs help us to organise our ideas and information so that our writing flows and makes sense to the reader.

❑ Paragraphs are not just sections of writing put into text in a haphazard way. They:

  – are a way of grouping ideas
  – put your text into order or sequence
  – should follow on from one another using the appropriate linking words.

❑ Paragraphs are themselves structured units of writing, often introduced by a topic sentence.

❑ Paragraphs can be arranged under headings in some types of text, for example information text.

❑ Each paragraph starts with an introductory sentence, then the rest of the paragraph is either about the introductory sentence or supports it.

HANDOUT 52

The task

In Session 5 you looked for some information in childcare textbooks. Your tutor has photocopied that information for you.

- Your task is to write a summary of what the text is about. Your summary must be at least three paragraphs long.
- Use the skills you have developed throughout the Basic Skills sessions.

Step 1 – plan
Step 2 – draft
Step 3 – proof-read and make any corrections and changes
Step 4 – final draft

There are lots of handouts that you and your tutor will go through together to help you with this activity. Use the handouts on 'Planning writing' from Session 6 and the handout on 'Paragraphs' from earlier in this session as well.

There are some writing frames for you to use if you want to on Handout 55.

When you have planned, drafted and proof-read, and you are sure that your work is OK, you can copy out your final draft. Your tutor will then check and mark it for you.

Editing your first draft

Writing a first draft can be helpful as:

✓ You can get your ideas and thoughts onto paper quickly, without too much worrying about spelling.

✓ You can do it in rough and alter anything you don't like.

✓ You can change things around later if you want to. You may want to take a break between drafting and editing, it may help to see things more clearly.

✓ You can check your draft for order, spelling, meaning, grammar, etc. and change anything you are unhappy with.

✓ When you have finished your first draft, read it through to check:

- You have written what you meant to say.
- It suits your purpose and audience.
- It makes sense to you and will do to others.
- You have included everything you wanted to.
- Style and format are OK.

As you do this, underline any spellings you are unsure of and check them before making your final draft. Alter anything you want/need to.

HANDOUT 54

Proof-reading

You have edited your first draft and made all the changes necessary. Now you need to proof-read it.

It is best not to do this straight away – wait a while and look at it later with fresh eyes.

When proof-reading you are checking for:

✓ Spelling
✓ Punctuation
✓ Grammar

so it's really time to put all those new found skills to good use!

Proof-reading is not easy and it does take time; however, it makes for a much better 'finished product' and shows you care about your work.

When proof-reading:

✓ Read in detail – do not skim
✓ Put yourself in the reader's place
✓ Look for one type of error at a time, e.g. spelling, then punctuation, etc.
✓ If you are writing to a deadline, leave plenty of time for proof-reading and editing
✓ Ask someone else to proof-read your work as well.

© June Green (2003) *Basic Skills for Childcare – Literacy*. Published by David Fulton Publishers Ltd.

Planning sheet

Below is a reminder of some strategies you can use to plan your writing.

WRITING PLAN

➤ What is my task?
➤ Set criteria are?
➤ Who is it for?
➤ Style? (formal/informal/technical)
➤ Format? (essay, list, bullet points)
➤ What do I need to include?

WRITING FRAME

You have been asked to summarise some text in at least three paragraphs.

➤ What will you put where?
➤ First paragraph?
➤ Second paragraph?
➤ Third paragraph?

Well done – you are now ready to make your first draft.

Speaking and Listening activities for Entry Level Three

> For these activities you will need:
>
> - A variety of children's poetry and verse.
> - A tape recorder.
> - Baby bathing equipment and a 'baby'.

Activity 1

Explain to students that you are going to demonstrate how to bath a baby, after which they will be expected to do it themselves. Tell them that during the demonstration you will expect students to acknowledge that they understand what they have to do. They should do this using verbal and non-verbal language.

When you have finished ask some questions to check everyone knows what to do.

Next give students a 'message' about a visit from the external moderator. The message should include date and time of visit, work the moderator wants to see, any instructions about the work, e.g. when it should be given in to you, names of any students the moderator wants to interview and times of their appointment. When finished, ask questions to check students have got all the detail.

Have a short group discussion on the two sets of instructions. Which were easier to follow and why? Did they need to listen for detail? In which message was it more important to listen to detail and why?

Activity 2

Tell students you are compiling a tape of poems to be used with children at a nursery. Each of them has to read out a poem/verse clearly and with expression, for recording onto the tape.

Activity 3

Students need to get into pairs for this role-play activity. They should choose between them who will be a parent and who will be a classroom assistant. Ask them to imagine one of the children had a slight accident at lunchtime and bumped his head. The classroom assistant has to explain the following to the parent/carer when he/she picks the child up at the end of the day:

- How and when the accident happened
- What treatment was given

- How the child has been since the accident
- What signs/symptoms the parent/carer should watch out for.

The 'parent' should have a couple of questions ready to ask. Make sure that everyone takes a turn at being the classroom assistant and the parent.

Activity 4

Hold a group discussion around the following topic: 'Smacking children – should it be allowed or not?' Each student is expected to take part in the discussion, both as a speaker and as a listener.

CHAPTER 5

Level One

Introduction

At this level we will be looking at:

- texts from a variety of sources
- the type of language these texts use, sentence structure and layout
- how to locate and identify specific information in texts
- writing to communicate ideas and opinions
- using length, format and style appropriate to the content and audience
- use of pronouns, commas, apostrophes and inverted commas
- more prefixes and suffixes
- spelling homophones of more than one syllable.

Reading will be the primary focus of the first session. The more text formats and styles students are introduced to when reading, the more they will be able to apply to their own writing and the more varied their writing will be. During the first few sessions students will be reinforcing their dictionary skills as they try to find meanings of unfamiliar words, many of which will be related to their childcare course.

SESSION 1

For this session you will need:

- Photocopies of text from childcare and education books.
- Highlighter pens.
- Enough dictionaries for each student to work from individually during this session.
- Copies of some childcare glossaries that must contain the words *stereotype, identify, list, describe, analyse, evaluate* and *explain*.

Activities

Activity 1 Introduction

- Start by explaining to students what they will be covering in Level One. Talk about how the content relates to skills covered in previous levels.
- Point out that all courses of study have their own specialist language and that childcare is no exception. It is important to understand what these 'technical' words mean. There are two main sources of information for establishing word meanings – dictionaries and glossaries.
- Give out copies of Handout 56, 'Dictionaries and glossaries' and ask students to complete the exercise. (It would be helpful at this point to distribute copies of the 'How to use a dictionary' handout that you looked at in Session 5 of Entry Level Two (Handout 30).)
- Once everyone in the group has finished discuss responses and talk about the differences between glossaries and dictionaries.
- Give out copies of Handout 57, 'What's the difference?' and ask students to do the stereotype activity at the bottom of the sheet. Take feedback and discuss responses when they have finished.
- End the activity by explaining to students that glossaries like the ones they'll find in their course books are written in a particular context – in this case, childcare. Therefore the definition of the word will be given in a childcare context. Dictionaries on the other hand have a far wider use. Everyone uses them, so the definitions they give need to be more general. In addition, dictionaries often give more than one meaning, they will tell you what part of speech the word is, e.g. a noun, and will provide any other relevant information that will help you to use the word.

Activity 2 Focus exercise

Rw/
L1.1, 2

Give out copies of Activity Sheet 42, 'Assignment jargon!' and ask students to complete the exercise. Take feedback from the activity once everyone has finished.

Activity 3 Focus exercise

Give out the texts you photocopied from childcare books before the session started. Ask students to read through them and highlight unfamiliar words, making a list of them as they go along. They should then look up the meaning of these words in a dictionary or glossary and record them in their Workbooks.

Activity 4 **Explanation/focus exercise**

Now students know the meanings of the unfamiliar words they highlighted in Activity 3 they need to begin using them in their own writing. Ask students to write a sentence that incorporates each of the words they looked up in the previous activity. Explain that they need to try and use each word in a sentence that will help them remember it. For example, 'I will *explain* to the child by *giving* him *clear details about what to do.*'

Activity 5 **Focus exercise/group discussion**

- Give each student a copy of Activity Sheet 43, 'What goes where?' and ask them to fill in the missing words as instructed on the sheet.
- Discuss answers as a group (these have been provided for you in Figure 5.1). Point out that a number of factors, including the title, context, knowledge of verb/tense and subject–verb agreement, will have helped them put the right words in place.

Tutor's answers to 'What goes where?' activity

Child development

It is <u>important</u> for childcare workers to know how <u>children</u> develop. There are five areas of child development. They are:

1. cognitive
2. <u>language</u>
3. social
4. emotional
5. <u>behaviour</u>

Childcare workers need to know and <u>understand</u> how children develop because:

- they need to prepare <u>activities</u> that are suitable for children of different ages
- they need to know what children should be capable of at different <u>ages</u>
- they need to be able to <u>identify</u> any potential problems the child might have.

Figure 5.1 Answers to exercise on Activity Sheet 43

Activity 6 **Focus exercise**

End the session with 'A fearsome tale' activity which should appeal to students! Start by giving a copy of Activity Sheet 44 to each member of the group and read the tale aloud to the class. Put as much expression and atmosphere into it as possible and ask the students to follow the text as you read.

Together discuss the questions at the bottom of the sheet and see if the students can transform the text into a cheerful tale by changing some of the words.

H A N D O U T   5 6

Dictionaries and glossaries

A *dictionary* is a book that consists of words set out in alphabetical order with their meanings and any other relevant information. There are also language dictionaries and spelling dictionaries.

A *glossary* is a list of 'technical' or 'specialist' words set out in alphabetical order with an explanation of each of them. It is found in a book that concentrates on the particular speciality, e.g. childcare. You have one in your literacy Workbooks.

Below are some words you might come across or already have seen during your childcare course.

Look them up in your dictionary and glossary and write out the meanings in the table below.

WORD	DICTIONARY DEFINITION	GLOSSARY DEFINITION
Asthma		
Development		
Neglect		
Nutrients		
Play		

How different are the meanings?

H A N D O U T   5 7

What's the difference?

In the last activity you will have noticed that glossaries and dictionaries are different in the following ways:

* How they are set out
* The amount of information they give

A *glossary* will be found in a specialist book, usually at the back or front of it. It is a list of specialist words and phrases with a definition of what they mean. Its only similarity to a dictionary is that the words are listed in alphabetical order.

A *dictionary* is a book full of words and their meanings. It does not contain specialist words alone: the words are from the written and spoken language, in this case English.

Along with the definition, dictionaries also include information about the word itself:

* Type of word
* Other forms of the word
* Derivatives of the word
* All of its meanings – if it has more than one

Look back at the 'How to use a dictionary' handout from Entry Level Two to remind you!

ACTIVITY

Look up the word 'stereotype' in the glossary and dictionary you have been given. Make a note of the differences for a discussion. Which of the definitions would be of most use to you if you were completing a childcare assignment?

Assignment jargon!

Listed below are words that you will come across when you are completing course assignments. To complete the assignment successfully you need to know them and understand what they mean.

✳ Go through the list and write down what you think they mean.

✳ When you have done that look up the meanings in a dictionary and glossary. How different are the definitions? Which would be more useful to you during your course?

List	Identify
Describe	Evaluate
Explain	Analyse

ACTIVITY SHEET 43

What goes where?

Written below are two pieces of text each with some words missing. Fill in the gaps with one of the words from the list below.

Child development

It is . . . . for childcare workers to know how . . . . develop. There are five areas of child development. They are:

1. cognitive
2. . . . .
3. social
4. emotional
5. . . . .

Childcare workers need to know and . . . . how children develop because:

• they need to prepare . . . . that are suitable for children of different ages

• they need to know what children should be capable of at different . . . .

• they need to be able to . . . . any potential problems the child might have.

behaviour	**training**	**unimportant**	**area**
important	**workers**	**children**	**prepare**
identify	**develop**	**problems**	**suitable**
language	**capable**	**understand**	**allergies**
activities	**centile-charts**	**development**	**ages**
watch	**hygiene**	**play**	**records**

Rw/L1.2

A fearsome tale

We woke up on this dark, deserted island. The sky was pitch black and darkness was all around us. The wind was blowing wildly and the trees were making loud rustling noises that sounded like someone or something was creeping around.

In the distance we could hear chanting and animal-like howling. It was carried to us on the wild wind. There was a red glow in the sky. Was some awful sacrifice going on?

How we got here is a mystery, none of us can remember. All we can remember is the feeling of dread when the storm came, the crashing of huge waves and the boat going up and down. The fearful shouts of the sailors and the terror in their voices will remain with us always.

Which words make this a scary tale?

What effect do these words have on the reader? Can you replace them with other words that would make this into a nicer tale?

Outline

The focus of this session is word work. Building on the skills covered in the previous sessions, students will be analysing word structure, how words relate to one another, root words, prefixes and suffixes, and building sentences.

For this session you will need:

- A selection of texts minus their headings from a variety of sources, including childcare books, romantic novels, crime stories, advertisements, instructions, indexes from different books, weather and sport reports. You will need enough for each student to have a selection to work from.
- Enough dictionaries for each student to work from individually if necessary.
- Highlighter pens.

Activities

Activity 1   Introduction

- Remind students that in the last session they looked at a piece of 'fearsome' text and used some words to change its tone. These words are called 'descriptive words'.
- Explain that there are many types of words in the English language. Give out copies of Activity Sheet 45, 'Where would I find these words?' and ask students to complete the exercise.
- Discuss answers (these are provided for you in Figure 5.2). Point out that different word types are found in different sorts of text, for example you wouldn't expect to find 'sloppy' romantic words in a horror story or to see 'sci-fi' language in an advert for shampoo! This knowledge is useful when we are trying to work out words and their meanings.
- Arrange students into pairs. Ask every student to pick one word from each of the texts they have looked at and use it in a sentence of their own. The sentence should be complete and grammatically correct. Ask them to discuss with their partner where they could use this sentence and why.

Activity 2   Explanation

- Another strategy for working out meanings is the knowledge that some words are related to each other. Write the following example for the group on the flipchart:

comfort means a state of physical well-being

comfortable means provides or gives comfort

uncomfortable means causes discomfort

- All these words belong to the '*comfort*' family, i.e. *comfort* is the root word.
- Give out copies of Handout 58, 'Word families' and go through it with the students. Ask the group to complete the activity at the bottom of the sheet.

Tutor's answer sheet for 'Where would I find these words?' activity

Romantic novel	Crime story	Hair product advertisement
love	police	shiny
affection	forensic	clean
kiss	detective	fresh
lover	victim	conditioner

Chocolate advert	Instructions	Child development book
creamy	when	language
smooth	after	age
milk	next	stage
melts	then	skills

Course assignment

investigate
explain
write
identify

Figure 5.2 Answers to exercise on Activity Sheet 45

- Explain that some prefixes can give clues as to word meanings. For example:
  - The prefix *bi* means two, having two, occurring or lasting for two, occurring twice or both sides.
  - The word *lingual* means expressed with the tongue or language.
  - The word *bilingual* means able to speak two languages or expressed in two languages.

- Give out copies of Activity Sheet 46, 'Prefix this!' and add a prefix to one of the words as an example. Ask students to complete the rest.

Activity 3 Focus exercise   Rt/L1.2

Give out the texts with no titles on. Ask students to go through them and judge where they came from and what they are about. Look for clues such as language style, format of text, presentation, pictures, etc. Discuss feedback once everyone in the group has finished.

Activity 4   Group discussion

Language style can also reflect the purpose of text. Together have a look at Handout 59, 'Which is which?'. Explain to the students that one is an objective description and the other is a persuasive description. Discuss which of them is which. How can the students tell?

During the discussion make the following points:

- Objective writing uses only factual language.
- Persuasive writing uses a lot of language that will persuade the reader about something.

Finish by talking about the differences between the types of words used.

Activity 5   Group discussion

Ask students to go through the two texts used in the last activity and highlight the main points in each. When they have done that discuss the following as a group:

- What were the main points?
- Which parts added detail to the main points?
- If you left them out, which parts wouldn't change the meaning of the text?
- Were there any sentences that needed reading more than once before the meaning became clear?
- Is there anything in the text that is suggestive rather than objective?

Activity 6   Idea storm

As this session has focused primarily on reading, this is a good time to encourage students to start reading more!

- Idea storm thoughts about what sort of texts people read for pleasure. Write suggestions on the board. These might include the following:

- Ask students to think about a type of book they would like to read for pleasure and take them to the library to choose a reading book.
- Discuss the reading diaries that are in their Workbooks.

Where would I find these words?

Below is a list of words of different types.

What type of text would you see them in? (List them on a separate piece of paper, under the headings below)

investigate   age   love   police   next

fresh   smooth   affection   stage

write   victim   detective   clean   explain   lover

language   identify   when   shiny

kiss   forensic   after   melts   then

creamy   milk   skills   conditioner

❏ Romantic novel

❏ Crime story

❏ Hair product advertisement

❏ Chocolate advert

❏ Instructions

❏ Child development book

❏ Course assignment

Rt/
L1.1, 2, 3
Rw/
L1.2, 3

HANDOUT 58

Word families

Word families are groups of words that go together because they have the same root word. Prefixes and suffixes are added to the root words to make them into different words.

Word families are usually found in the same types of texts. Recognising word families is a good strategy for spelling and finding meaning.

Two word families you may have come across during your childcare course are:

develop	play

develop*ment* play*ing*
develop*ing* play*ful*
develop*ed* *dis*play

ACTIVITY

Which prefixes or suffixes could you add to the root words below?

grow	paint	report
able	plan	ability

Can you work out what the words in the word families mean? If not look them up in a dictionary. Can you think of any other word families?

Prefix this!

Below are a list of root words and a list of prefixes. Add a prefix to the root word and try working out what it means.

Look up the meaning of the root word before you start if you are unsure of what it means.

ROOT WORDS

cycle	school
colour	angle
date	happy
hurt	do
mature	annual
lateral	

Prefixes and their meanings:

* **Bi** = two, having two, occurring or lasting two, occurring twice, on both sides

* **Tri** = three, thrice, occurring every three

* **Pre** = before in time or in position

* **Un** = reversal of an action, removal from

HANDOUT 59

Which is which?

Below are two different types of text. One is an objective text,
the other is a persuasive text. Which is which and how can you tell?

TEXT 1

Blue Lakes is a beautiful island in the Mediterranean. It is a small, quiet and beautifully kept island where the inhabitants are friendly and welcoming. There are no loud noisy bars and discos here, yet the island does not lack sources of entertainment. There are lovely restaurants where fresh seafood dishes are served, the likes of which is so fresh you can almost taste the sea. For youngsters there is the 'tots centre' where visitors' children can meet and play together with the children who live on the island. What better way for young children to pick up a few words of another language!

Life on the island has an easy, calm and restful pace. The warm sunshine, the blue, blue lakes and the peaceful pine-tree woods make this one of the most scenic places in the Mediterranean. Wander around at your leisure, eat fresh food, mix with local people and enjoy the rest and relaxation. You are sure to enjoy Blue Lakes and want to come back for more.

TEXT 2

'Splash Time' is a new water play centre just opened, situated within the 'Funtime Leisure Park' in Sandholme.

Within the centre are a variety of water features, six different swimming pools and a family pool. All water areas are closely supervised by well-trained and experienced personnel, all of whom are qualified first aiders, and each water area is supervised by at least three lifeguards at any one time; more at peak activity times.

Also within the centre are two restaurants. There is the Lakeview restaurant with its own A La Carte menu for people wanting a quiet evening meal. The restaurant has a view of the outdoor lake, which is lit up at night.

For those wanting a family meal there is the Poolview restaurant. This restaurant serves a variety of meals and has a special children's menu. The Poolview overlooks the fountain theme pool, so you can watch the fountains and see people enjoying themselves in the pool. There are also a variety of activities in the children's playroom which is supervised by qualified childcare workers.

For further information or to book a meal call us on 0976 421355.

SESSION 3

Outline

In this session students have an opportunity to use the reading techniques they learnt during Entry Level Three to find information and explore sentences within different types of text.

> For this session you will need:
>
> - Local bus timetables for buses to college and some other routes.
> - A large selection of texts, including holiday brochures, instructions, leaflets, film or TV guides, childcare texts, assignments, maths and science texts. Some of them should contain images.
> - Different coloured highlighter pens.
> - Books for children of various ages.

Activities

Activity 1 Introduction

- Recap skimming, scanning and detailed reading techniques covered in Session 4 of Entry Level Three. Give out copies of Handout 45, 'Reading' (p. 160) to jog a few memories.
- Hand out copies of Activity Sheet 47, 'Getting to town' and explain the activity to the students. Ask them to complete it using the three reading techniques you have just revised.
- When the students have finished, discuss how they found the information using the reading techniques.

Activity 2 Focus exercise

Arrange students into twos and give each pair a selection of texts from the range you collected before the start of the session. Make sure each pair has a copy of Activity Sheet 48, 'Different text types' and ask them to explore the variety of texts you have given them and complete the activities on the sheet.

When the pairs have completed the exercise discuss their answers as a group.

Activity 3 Group discussion

- Start by recapping verb tenses, nouns, adjectives and adverbs.
- Ask students to highlight some examples of each of these parts of speech in the texts they explored earlier.
- Have a whole-class discussion about the examples they have found. Do any of these word types appear more in one type of text than another? Students may have noticed that verbs and adverbs appear most frequently in instructional text. Point out that this is because both sorts are doing and action words!
- Give out copies of Handout 60, 'Making a meringue' and read through it together, [Rs/L1.1] identifying the verbs and adverbs in the text. What effect do the adverbs have on what's written? Point out that the adverbs tell us *how* to carry out the actions (the verbs), e.g. '*carefully* separate', '*fiercely* whisk', '*gently* fold'.

- To round off the activity give students a blank sheet of flipchart and ask them to come up with a sentence that uses a noun, a verb, an adjective and an adverb. Ask them to highlight or write each part of speech in a different colour.

Activity 4 Discussion

Give out copies of Handout 61, 'Then and now' to the group. In pairs, ask students to discuss which is a narrative and which is a description. How can they tell? Encourage them to discuss the features of each text.

Take feedback from the group. Here are a few points worth mentioning:

- '*Then*' as a title gives you a clue that this text is about something that has happened. It is written in the past tense: *had, chattered, met up in the car park*, etc.
- '*Now*' as a title gives a clue that this is about something happening now, a description. It is written in the present tense: *is, playing, carrying*, etc.
- Both texts are about children.

Working in pairs, see if the students can pick out the words that are used a lot in both texts. When they have done that ask them to identify the verbs and to say whether they are past, present or future tense.

Activity 5 Explanation

As with writing we use punctuation to help us make sense of what we are reading.

- Recap the sorts of punctuation that are used to mark the end of a sentence – full stops, question marks, exclamation marks and so on – all of which have already been covered in previous levels.
- Explain to the group that two other punctuation marks that they are likely to come across on a regular basis are COMMAS and APOSTROPHES.
- Give out copies of Handout 62, 'Commas' and Handout 63, 'Apostrophes' and go through them with the students.
- Ask students to read through the handouts a second time and then to look again at the *Then* and *Now* texts (Handout 61), this time identifying commas and apostrophes.
- Take feedback from the students once they have completed the exercise.

Activity 6 Focus exercise

Students should work in pairs for this activity. Using the various texts explored at the beginning of the session, ask learners to complete the exercises on Activity Sheet 49, 'Exploring texts'.

Encourage the pairs to discuss their answers in front of the group once they have all finished.

Activity 7 Reflection

End the session with a discussion on what the students feel they have learned from exploring the different types of text. In preparation for the following session, ask how they think this might help them in their own writing.

For the next session ask students to bring in a word they have had trouble spelling. Stress that it doesn't matter whether they can spell it now or not!

Getting to town

Your study group needs to do some research about prices of baby equipment for a course project. To do this you need to visit some shops in the town centre. You have arranged to meet at 10.30 a.m. in town. To get there you need to catch a bus from outside the college.

- What time do you want to get to town?
- Which bus do you need to catch?
- What time do you need to catch the bus?
- What time will it get you into town?
- If you wanted to have a half-hour coffee stop before meeting them what time would you need to get on the bus?

Rt/L1.3

ACTIVITY SHEET 48

Different text types

You have been given a variety of text types. In pairs look through them and discuss the following:

✳ Which ones can you just read the main points and know what it is telling you?

✳ Which would you need to read in detail to understand?

In the texts that contain images:

✳ What do the images add to the text?

✳ Are they essential to the meaning and purpose of the text?

✳ Do any of the images give additional information to the text?

Making a meringue

You will need:

3 large eggs
¾ cup castor sugar

Method

Carefully separate the egg yolks and egg whites.

Fiercely whisk the egg whites until they form stiff peaks.

Beat in two tablespoons of the sugar and continue beating until the peaks are very stiff and glossy.

Using a metal spoon gently fold the rest of the sugar into the mixture.

When you have carefully folded in the rest of the sugar, the meringue is ready to use.

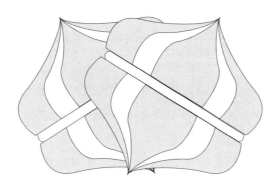

HANDOUT 61

Then and now

Then

The children had looked forward to the trip. As they got on the bus they chattered excitedly to each other about what they would see when they got there.

"I bet we see a snake", said Timmy.

"And a frog", said Imran.

"There's going to be lots of things to see", said the teacher.

"I'm sure we'll have lots of fun", she told them.

When they got to the bog they gathered together to listen to their teacher. She told them which group they would be in. They collected their plastic pots and boxes and off they went.

At three o'clock they all met up in the car park near the bog. While they waited for the bus to come they chattered about what they had seen, and showed each other the tadpoles and other things they had collected.

When the bus came they climbed on and sat down in their seats. The teacher made sure everyone was present and off they went back to school.

When they got back to school, the teacher put the children's tadpoles into the pond at the end of the playground.

Now

The teacher has decided to give the children some outdoor time. It has been a busy week and they have worked hard.

The children are playing in the playground. There is a variety of equipment available, for example bikes, balls, a climbing frame and a seesaw.

Some children are playing on the equipment while others are playing a game of tig. Two girls are sitting on the grass and appear to be deep in conversation.

The teacher comes outside carrying a box of ice-lollies and calls the children to her. The children each take a lolly and sit down on the grass to eat it.

Commas

You will see commas used quite a lot in text that you read.

> The comma (,) has a few uses.

1. To show a short pause in a sentence, for example: *Lynsey wants to go bowling, but Talvinder wants to go shopping.*

2. To separate the introductory phrase from the main part of the sentence, for example: *After a few weeks of hard work, the students are looking forward to the half-term break.*

3. When words such as 'therefore' or 'however' are used to show how a train of thought is developing, a comma should be used to mark them off, for example: *There has been poor response to the invitations; therefore, the trip to the theatre has been cancelled.*

4. A comma can be used to separate items in a list, for example: *The children will need a waterproof jacket, wellingtons, a packed lunch and some spending money.*

5. Commas are used to separate the name of a person or people being spoken to in the rest of the sentence, for example: *Thank you, children, for being so helpful.*

6. A comma is used to separate words in quotation/speech marks from the rest of the sentence, for example: *"I like painting", said Margaret.*

HANDOUT 63

Apostrophes

When reading, you will sometimes see apostrophes used in the text.

> The apostrophe (') has two uses.

1. To show possession (the 'possessive' apostrophe), for example: *Samreen's assignment, Roswana's observation* or *the children's books.*

   As you can see, in these examples the apostrophe is added at the end of the name, followed by an 's'. This shows us that the assignment belongs to Samreen, the observation belongs to Roswana and the books belong to the children.

   If you want to add an apostrophe to a plural word that already ends in an 's' the apostrophe is added after the 's', for example: *The students' classroom* or *The teachers' staffroom.*

2. An apostrophe can also be used to show that a letter is missing (the 'omissive' apostrophe).

   It shows something has been omitted, for example: "Who's missing today?" instead of "Who is missing today?" and "What's that?" instead of "What is that?"

   In both cases the 'i' has been left out.

   Another example is *fish'n'chips* or *rock'n'roll.* In these two examples the letters 'a' and 'd' have been left out.

The omissive apostrophe should only be used in informal writing, for example an email to a friend or a chatty letter. If you were writing a letter of application you would not use it.

Exploring texts

You will need the different texts you have explored in this session for these activities.

☺ Choose one piece of text and ask your partner to find some information from it. Your partner will present the information to you. Have they missed anything out? Is all the information given relevant to what you wanted?

☺ With your partner compare the following in the texts:
  • Informal/formal style
  • Technical language and use of adverbs
  • Sentence length and type

☺ Now look at the punctuation marks in the text. Are omissive apostrophes used anywhere? Are they used in any particular type of text? What are commas used for?

☺ Highlight any specialist or technical language that is used. Using your own knowledge of sentence structure, word patterns and context try and predict what they mean.

☺ Check out their meanings in a dictionary and put them into your Workbook.

SESSION 4

Outline

Having spent a number of sessions on reading, the next few sessions will focus primarily on writing. It is hoped that the reading work done earlier in the level will influence and enrich the students' own writing.

In this session the students will be exploring some spelling rules and more punctuation marks.

Activities

Activity 1 **Introduction**

Open the session with a whole-class discussion to find out how students are getting on with their spelling and to share any strategies they have found particularly useful.

Activity 2 **Explanation**

In the English language there are lots of words that sound the same (or very similar) but are spelt differently and have different meanings. These words are called HOMOPHONES.

Write 'here' and 'hear' on the board as an example. Can students think of any others? Give out copies of Handout 64, 'Common homophones' and go through it with the students.

Ww/L1.1 **Activity 3** **Focus exercise**

In pairs, students should be given one or two sets of common homophones and a copy of Activity Sheet 50, 'Using homophones'. You might like to provide them with an example before asking them to complete the exercise on the sheet, e.g. 'There are enough sweets *for four* children' and 'Today I'm going *to* visit *two* of my friends and my grandparents *too*.' They should use a dictionary to check any word meanings they are unsure of.

Take feedback once all the students have finished writing their sentences.

Activity 4 **Explanation**

Knowing spelling rules helps us enormously with our spelling and writing and there are quite a few of them to remember! One thing that many people get confused with is whether or not to double letters when adding a suffix, and another is how to alter the ending when changing a word from singular to plural. The rest of this session will be spent looking at these two rules.

- Give out copies of Handout 65, 'More suffixes' and go through it with the students, looking at the examples at the bottom of the sheet. Explain to them that in some cases suffixes can simply be added to the end of complete words, as in the examples on the handout. In other cases rules need to be followed.
- Give out copies of Handout 66, 'Adding to words' and go through the rules together.
- In pairs, ask each student to think of two words that their partner has to add a suffix to. They should write these down so that you can check their answers at the end.

Ww/L1.1

Common homophones

There are quite a few words in the English language that sound the same or similar, but are spelt differently and mean different things. We need to try and use the right spelling for our writing to make sense. Below is a list of some that are used most often.

* there/they're/their

* wear/where/were/we're

* to/two/too

* hear/here

* flour/flower

* tale/tail

* for/four

* affect/effect

* of/off

* you're/your

ACTIVITY SHEET 50

Using homophones

You have been given one or two sets of homophones. Taking one homophone at a time, write a sentence that uses it correctly.

Can you come up with a way to remember how to spell each of the homophones you have been given that will help you to use it correctly?

More suffixes

Before we look at rules for adding suffixes and changing words to plurals, there are some more suffixes you need to know about.

Here they are:

-al	*-ary*
-ship	*-ness*
-ible	*-able*
-tion	*-sion*

Here are some examples of how they can be used:

development + *-al* = developmen*tal*

wash + *-able* = wash*able*

member + *-ship* = member*ship*

kind + *-ness* = kind*ness*

HANDOUT 66

Adding to words

> If you know about rules for changing words it can help you to spell correctly.
>
> The two things that people get most confused with are:
>
> ➤ Doubling letters when adding a suffix.
> ➤ Changing a word from singular to plural.

Let's take a look at some rules that may help you.

✓ When adding a suffix that begins with a vowel to a one-syllable word, you double the consonant if there is one vowel before it.

Examples: tap – tapping   hot – hotter   rob – robbed

✓ If the one-syllable word has two vowels before the consonant, or ends in two consonants, you just add the suffix.

Examples: sleep – sleeping   cook – cooked   pack – package

Some words with more than one syllable follow the rule but others don't. Here's how it works for them:

✓ If the stress is on the first syllable in the word then there is one consonant before the suffix.
For example: offer – offering. Here the emphasis is on the *off* part of the word so there is one consonant (r) before the suffix.

✓ If the stress is on the second syllable in the word then there are two consonants before the suffix.
For example: propel – propelled. Here the stress is on the *pel* part of the word so there are two consonants (ll) before the suffix.

✓ Words ending with 'l' have a rule of their own – there's always one that has to be different! Words with more than one syllable, which end with one 'l' after a single vowel, always have the 'l' doubled.

For example: Travel – travelled or travelling
Pedal – pedalled or pedalling

Outline

This session should be spent working on the spelling rules introduced in the previous session. In the students' Workbooks there is a complete section covering all aspects of spelling rules (see 'Spelling rules' section on pp. 65–70). The section contains information and examples of all the rules that students need to be aware of.

It is a good idea to spend a whole session on this if possible. Spelling rules are an important part of literacy and warrant an entire session to themselves. Dealing with the topic in one go will maintain high interest levels and help promote greater understanding than exploring it bit by bit. The work can then be referred back to whenever necessary.

Activities

Activity 1   **Introduction**

Go through the rules listed on Handout 66, 'Adding to words' (p. 218) one by one, using the examples from the students' Workbooks.

Activity 2   **Focus exercise**

Ask students working in pairs or small groups to think about how the rules apply to other words. You might have to give them a selection of words to consider, or alternatively see if they can come up with a few of their own. Encourage them to keep referring back to Handout 66 as they do this.

Activity 3   **Focus exercise**

End the session with some fun team games or quizzes, using questions such as 'Change *baby* to its plural form' and 'Make *watch* into *watches*.'

SESSION 6

Outline

The object of this session is to increase students' confidence in writing in complete sentences and using punctuation. Much of it will involve revision of skills covered in previous sessions, but recapping in this way is never a bad thing. There will also be further opportunity for students to practise the spelling rules they looked at in Sessions 4 and 5.

Activities

Activity 1   Introduction

As a prelude to asking students to write their own sentences, spend some time recapping some of the spelling rules covered in previous sessions. Try and clear up any confusion or misunderstandings at the outset and encourage the students to ask about anything they are at all unsure of.

Activity 2   Focus exercise

Ws/L1.2

- Write the following words on the board: *baby, book, box, sleep, offer, boy, story, proper, toy, touch, tap, pedal.*
- Ask the students to write some sentences using these words in their plural forms. They can use more than one of the words in a sentence if they want to. When they have written a sentence they should check to see they have used the correct punctuation.
- Take feedback at the end of the activity. Were there any aspects of the exercise which students found particularly tricky? Why?

Activity 3   Explanation/focus exercise

- Recap punctuation marks and their uses with the group, paying particular attention to anyone who struggled in the previous activity.
- Explain to the students that the rest of the activity will require them to use a range of skills that they have acquired since they started work on Basic Skills Literacy.
- Give out copies of Activity Sheet 51, 'Writing for pleasure' and go through it with the students.
- Ask them to do the exercise individually. As this activity could take some time to complete, this is a good opportunity to introduce some word games such as Scrabble, Boggle or Upwords for those students who finish early. When everyone in the group has completed the task, take drafts and finished pieces of work in for marking. Having spent time and energy writing the texts on their own it will be important to the students to receive individual feedback on their work.

ACTIVITY SHEET 51

Writing for pleasure

Write a piece of text, approximately three paragraphs long, about one of the following:

☺ Explaining the letters A, B and C to young children
☺ Telling a new student about the course you are doing
☺ A reflective account about the last time you were at placement.

What to do:

1. Make a plan before you write it.
2. Draft it.
3. Proof-read to check spelling, subject–verb agreement, correct tense, correct use of plurals and correct use of punctuation before you hand it in to your tutor.
4. Make any necessary changes.
5. Hand in plans, first draft(s) and your finished piece of writing to your tutor for marking.

Remember:

✓ When planning think about how much to write, how much detail to put in, language style, putting your paragraphs into a logical sequence.
✓ The opening sentence of a paragraph tells the reader about the paragraph.

© June Green (2003) *Basic Skills for Childcare – Literacy*. Published by David Fulton Publishers Ltd.

SESSION 7

Outline

This session builds on skills covered in the previous two sessions, including writing in complete sentences and using plurals. If possible make some time in this session to see learners and give individual feedback on their writing from the last session. In the meantime students should use this time to be going through their Workbooks, doing any incomplete work, updating reading diaries, revising spelling rules, etc. Alternatively some members of the group may wish to use the time for private reading.

Activities

Activity 1   Introduction

- Remind students that in Entry Level Two, as part of their work on compound sentences, they explored conjunctions or 'linking' words. Recap what they are and see if they can remember the following: *and, however, but, then, so, also, when, because* and *therefore.*
- Give out copies of Handout 67, 'More conjunctions' and ask the students to have a go at the activity at the bottom of the sheet.
- As an extension to this, ask students to complete the 'Using conjunctions' exercise on Activity Sheet 52.
- Take feedback from the students about both of the activities – compare the two together as a group.

Activity 2   Explanation/focus exercise

Recap subject–verb agreement and verb tenses. Remind students that these are important grammatical strategies and need to be used so that our writing makes sense. Can they remember the following rules?

- Singular subjects have singular verbs
- Plural subjects have plural verbs
- Tense should be the same throughout a piece of writing.

This is a good time to remind students that when proof-reading their work they should keep an eye out for grammatical inaccuracies.

Wt/L1.6
Ws/L1.3

Round off the activity by giving out copies of Activity Sheet 53, 'Bring the past to the future'. Tell the students that they are now going to concentrate on tense work and that you would like them to change the text on the sheet from past to future tense. They should work individually for this activity.

Activity 3 Group discussion

Explain to the students that while you have been doing lots of work on writing accurately and in complete sentences – both of which are incredibly important – there are times when brief notes or lists are enough and complete accuracy is not essential.

Discuss levels of correctness and accuracy needed in different types of writing. Write the following headings on the board and examine each in turn:

- Notes
- Lists
- Complete sentences
- Paragraphs.

HANDOUT 67

More conjunctions

Remember the conjunctions (linking words) you looked at in Entry Level Two (*and, however, but, then, so, also, when, because* and *therefore*)?

Here are a few more that you can use in your writing:

✓ If
✓ While
✓ Though
✓ Since

These conjunctions can be used to join two short sentences together so that your writing flows smoothly and makes sense.

ACTIVITY

Try joining some of these sentences with these:

The children were very quiet.   ***when***

The teacher read a story.

Steve pushed Trish.   ***since***   ***if***

Trish hit Steve.

Tal finds numeracy hard.

She finds literacy easy.   ***though***

We cannot go to the park.   ***so***

It is raining hard.

The children went home.   ***while***

Playgroup was over.

Using conjunctions

Below is a list of instructions for carrying out a child observation. Rewrite them in paragraph format using conjunctions to join some sentences together.

<u>Instructions for carrying out a child observation</u>

1. Decide which child/children you will observe.
2. Decide what you will observe the child/children doing.
3. Set an aim for the observation.
4. Decide when you would like to carry out the observation.
5. Ask permission from placement mentor/supervisor.
6. Decide how you will record the observation.
7. Decide what format you will use to present your findings.
8. Make sure you have everything you need.
9. Carry out the observation.
10. Read it through.
11. Make some conclusions from what you have observed.
12. Compare your observation/conclusions to theory.
13. Make some evaluations.
14. Make some recommendations.
15. Write it up.
16. Hand it in to be marked and graded.

Wt/L1.6
Ws/
L1.1, 2

ACTIVITY SHEET 53

Bringing the past to the future

Below is a piece of text written in the past tense. Rewrite it in the future tense, making sure you keep it grammatically correct.

Yesterday I took David to the park. It had been raining for three days and we needed to get out.

When we got to the park I took David out of his buggy. He was very excited and started to run and shout. I had taken a ball with me. We played catch and football.

We spent some time at the adventure playground. There were slides, climbing frames and some swings. David loved the swings! I spent ages pushing him to and fro.

When we had finished at the adventure playground, we went for a long walk around the park. We fed the ducks, ran in the fallen leaves and jumped in the puddles. We had a lot of fun.

We ended our walk at the café. We were both a bit hungry so we had a snack and a drink. It was a good afternoon out.

SESSION 8

Outline

Building on the sentence work done in previous sessions, the focus of this session is on writing text.

For this session you will need:

• A selection of blank memo sheets, faxes, minute records, observation sheets and child health records.

Activities

Activity 1 **Introduction**

• Recap briefly the activities from the previous session and focus in particular on the points you made in Activity 3, i.e. that different types of writing call for different approaches.
• Explain to students that when we write we do not always use the same format. It depends on what we are writing, the reason we are writing it and whom we are writing it for. We structure our writing to suit our purpose.
• Give out copies of Activity Sheet 54, 'Planning and drafting the format' and ask students to complete the exercise. Before they begin putting pen to paper explain that there are a few more things they need to consider when preparing to write. Give out copies of Handout 68, 'Writing style' and go through it together.

Activity 2 **Explanation/focus exercise**

Sometimes we need to add things to text to clarify or emphasise the meaning. Examples of such elements include drawings, diagrams, charts and tables.

• Give out copies of Handout 69, 'Adding to text' and go through all four examples with the group. Can they think of any further elements that can be added to texts to express meaning? (Photographs in newspapers, illustrations in children's storybooks, etc.)
• Tell students that it is time to have another go at poster making. Do they remember the alphabet posters they designed for children during Entry Level One? Explain that the posters you are asking them to design in this session will contain a combination of writing and pictures/diagrams. Give out copies of Activity Sheet 55, 'Making a poster' and go through the options with the students.

Activity 3 **Idea storm/group discussion**

Point out to the group that some of the writing we do, especially in the workplace or at placement, will use a pre-set format. Can students think of any they have used? Idea storm pre-set formats as a group and list these on the board. Suggestions might include the following:

- Accident reports
- Records
- Memos
- Minutes of meetings
- Faxes
- Child observation/assessment sheets
- Child health records.

Discuss how much detail would be needed for each. Can students identify where accuracy is important, and why?

Invite students to come and choose one or two items from the selection of blank memo sheets, faxes, minute records, observation sheets and child health records which you gathered together before the session started. Ask them to practise filling these in and check their work as they do so.

Wt/
L1.1, 2

Planning and drafting the format

Plan and draft outlines for each of the text types listed below. Your plan should include:

- Main points
- Order they will go in
- Length of finished text.

Remember to also think about the style you will write in, considering all the points discussed in the 'Writing style' handout.

Text types

1. Instructions on how to get to college from town, for someone who is new to the area.

2. A letter booking a trip for the playgroup children to a local farm.

3. The answer to this instruction: Describe the language development that takes place between the ages of two and four years.

4. A plan to do a craft activity with the children at placement. The plan must include the materials you will need.

5. An invitation to a party at your place!

You will need to bring these drafts to the next session.

HANDOUT 68

Writing style

Before we start writing there are a number of things we need to consider about the style of our text.

When we talk about style we are talking about a combination of:

* *Language* – formal or informal, general or technical
* *Syntax* – the relationship between words, phrases, sentences, rules and patterns of writing
* *Organisation* – what needs to go at the beginning, order of points to be made, etc.

The following will influence these choices:

* *Audience* – who will be reading this?
* *Purpose* – why am I writing this?
* *Context* – is it to give information, instructions, or just a chat?

In your reading you will have come across many styles of writing from text messages to course books for your studies. Use the knowledge you have gained from your reading to help you think about your writing.

Adding to text

The following are sometimes used within text to make meaning clearer or to explain something: tables, lists, drawings, diagrams.

Here are some examples:

TABLE *(Used in a child observation)*

The table below shows how many children could complete the tasks.

	Threw the ball to another child	Caught the ball	Threw ball into the bucket
Child A	✓	✗	✗
Child B	✓	✓	✗
Child C	✗	✓	✗
Child D	✓	✗	✓
Child E	✓	✓	✓

Out of five children observed, only one managed all three tasks.

LIST *(Used in a text on how to promote children's language development)*

An excellent activity to promote children's conversation skills is an interest table. The following themes can be used for this activity: favourite toys, items from home, photographs and items found on a nature walk.

OR

An excellent activity to promote children's conversation skills is an interest table. The following themes can be used for this activity:

- Favourite toys
- Items from home
- Photographs
- Items found on a nature walk.

DRAWINGS *(Used to show stages in learning to draw)*

At stage five, a child is able to draw a circle and add eyes, nose and mouth to represent a face.

DIAGRAM *(Used to show which way up something should be)*

Wt/L1.5

Making a poster

Choose one of the following to design a poster about:

❏ A poster advertising a school summer fair.
❏ A poster that explains the shapes square, circle and triangle to young children.

Your poster must include some writing and pictures or diagrams.

Plan and draft your poster here

SESSION 9

Outline

This aim of this final session is for students to finish off and pull together all the skills they have learnt during Level One. They will be given the task of planning, drafting, proof-reading and producing a final piece of writing. You would be right in thinking that this exercise is almost identical to the one featured at the end of Entry Level Three. This repetition is completely intentional, as it is only by following the process over and over again that students will become familiar with the pattern and use it confidently in their future writing.

Activities

Activity 1   Introduction

- Start by recapping the planning process that you covered at the end of Entry Level Three.
- Ask students to think about the different sorts of texts and writing approaches that they have looked at in Level One. Discuss the plans they made in the previous session (Activity Sheet 54) for writing different texts.
- Can they tell you what levels of accuracy would be needed for each one?

Activity 2   Explanation

- Explain to the group that once you have covered planning the next thing you need to do is start drafting your text – putting together the first copy of your writing. Your first draft is where you get your ideas down on paper and nothing that you do is set in stone: you can cross out, rearrange and make any changes you want to at this point. When you have done this you can make your first copy and proof-read it.
- Give out copies of Handout 70, 'Proof-reading' and ask students to do the activity at the bottom of the sheet.

Activity 3   Discussion/focus exercise

- Spend some time discussing with students the writing skills they have developed over the nine sessions in Level One. Explain that to end this level and bring together all they have learnt, you would like them to do a writing task.
- Before they begin they need to choose a topic on which to write. Give out copies of Activity Sheet 56, 'What shall I write about?' and point out that one of the easiest and most pleasurable things to write about is something that you enjoy or feel strongly about – a hobby or a favourite TV programme, for instance.
- Set aside some time before the students begin to write to discuss concerns and answer questions about this task. Some students may see it as a monumental task and be worried by it. This is the point at which to allay fears and build confidence!
- Decide between you how long the students are likely to need to complete this task, and set a deadline for them to work to.

Wt/L1.6

Proof-reading

When we proof-read we check our writing for a variety of things:

- ❏ Spelling errors
- ❏ Use of punctuation
- ❏ Omissions
- ❏ Repetitions
- ❏ Whether it makes sense to readers
- ❏ Legibility
- ❏ Usefulness to reader
- ❏ Level of detail
- ❏ Accuracy
- ❏ Grammar:
  - – Subject–verb agreement
  - – Use of tense
  - – Correct use of words, phrases and sentences.

ACTIVITY

Proof-read the text below, make any changes you think are necessary and rewrite it correctly.

Studying a childcare course are hard work. You has to go to college and learn about childrens you has to go to placement and work with them two. There is assignments to do. On all the subjects you is learned about

Child devlopment is abowt how childrens gro and develop their is a lot to lurn you has to observe children and write it. We learns about activities we can doo with the childrens and how to keeps them safe.

Wt/
L1.1–6
Ws/
L1.1–3

ACTIVITY SHEET 56

What shall I write about?

Choose from one of the following:

✳ a topic that interests you
✳ something you are knowledgeable about
✳ a hobby
✳ a book you have read
✳ a film or TV programme you have watched recently.

You are going to write an explanation about what you have chosen for someone who knows nothing about it. You have developed a lot of skills throughout the Basic Skills sessions, now is your chance to put them to work for you!

1. Plan your writing.
2. Draft your writing.
3. Write your first copy.
4. Proof-read it and make corrections.
5. Write a fresh final copy if you need to.
6. Hand in to your tutor to be marked.

Use the handouts you've been given in this and previous sessions about things to consider when planning, drafting and proof-reading.

GOAL

YOU CAN DO IT!

Speaking and Listening activities for Level One

> For these activities you will need:
>
> - A list of suitable local places for an end of school-year trip, for a Reception class.
>
> - A first aid video showing CPR and how to put someone in the recovery position. (You might choose to do your own demonstration instead.)

Activity 1

SLc/ L1.1, 2
SLd/ L1.1, 2, 3
SLlr/ L1.4, 5, 6

This activity should be done in small groups. The scenario is a meeting to discuss where to take the Reception class children for their end of school-year outing. Students need to discuss and decide the following: venue, date, transport, number of adults needed, cost to parents and whether any special facilities are required, e.g. wheelchair access.

> ➤ Everyone at the meeting should take part, displaying their listening skills and asking questions. They should also show that they are able to create opportunities to interrupt in an appropriate way.

Activity 2

SLc/ L1.3, 4
SLlr/ L1.1, 2, 3

The group needs to be divided in two for this activity. Half of the group should leave the room for their break while the other half watch the video/demonstration on CPR. When the others return ask them to pair up with someone who has watched the CPR demonstration. The students who have seen the demo should explain CPR to their classmates. Let the whole group then watch the video/demonstration together and discuss how effective the explanations were, if anything was missed out, etc.

The CPR group should then go for a break while the other half watch the recovery position demonstration. When the other students return repeat the activity as before.

Activity 3

SLlr/L1.3, 4, 5, 6
SLc/ L1.2, 3

This is a fun activity. Each student should think of a familiar famous person they would like to be. Without anyone seeing they should write the name of the person on a piece of paper and attach it to the back of someone else in the group.

The object is for each person to find out the name of the celebrity on his or her back by questioning others in the group. They should ask straightforward questions and receive straightforward answers. Students can only ask three questions of the same person. When they know who they have on their back they can sit down. Other people can still ask them questions.

CHAPTER 6

Level Two

Introduction

Here we are at Level Two. The students have certainly come a long way since their pre-Entry Level One introductory session. They have done an enormous amount of work and have gained lots of new skills along the way.

This final level is where you help them to tie everything up. Much of the work in the following nine sessions will seem somewhat repetitive and in a way it is; however, students are improving and growing as learners all the time, using and building on existing skills in new situations.

What you will notice as you read through the chapter is that whereas these skills were covered individually in previous levels, here they are built into activities and used more implicitly. You'll also notice that there are fewer explanatory handouts. This is to encourage students to listen to more complicated instructions and explanations directly from you.

Outline

The aim of this first session is to complete some of the topics that students made a start on in previous levels, for example pronouns, suffixes and prefixes, and exploring complex sentences.

For this session you will need:

- A variety of texts comprising simple and compound sentences. They could be from newspapers, magazines, textbooks or journals. Each text should be cut up into sentences and put into its own envelope. You will need enough sets for students to do a paired activity.
- Blank sheets of flipchart for the paired activity above.

Activities

Activity 1   Introduction

- Start by telling the students what they will be covering in this session. Explain that once they have dealt with these topics in the first few activities they will have completed the learning at word level and will then concentrate on putting it all into practice in their writing.
- Recap work done on prefixes and suffixes in Entry Level Three and Level One. Give each student a copy of Activity Sheet 57, 'More prefixes and suffixes' and go through the points on the sheet together before they complete the exercise. Remind the students about the rules for changing words which they looked at in Session 4 of Level One (see Handout 66, 'Adding to words' on p. 218).
- Take feedback once the students have completed the activity.

Activity 2   Explanation/focus exercise

- Move on now to pronouns, recapping what they are and why they are used. (Look back at the work done on nouns in Session 6 of Entry Level Two, where students touched on the subject of pronouns when they read through Handout 31, 'Naming nouns'.)
- Give out copies of Handout 71, 'More about pronouns' and have a look at the activities at the bottom of the sheet. Start by asking if any of them can think of any more examples of any of the different pronoun types. When you have finished discussing this ask the learners to write some sentences, each one incorporating a different type of pronoun.
- Take feedback from the group once all the students have finished writing.

Activity 3   Focus exercise

To reinforce the word level work done in Activities 1 and 2 give each student a copy of Activity Sheet 58, 'Word games' and ask the group to have a go at the activities. A 'missing homophone' exercise has been thrown in for good measure and might come as a surprise to some of the students. Jog a few memories if necessary by writing a brief example on the board: 'Come over *here* so that you can *hear* me better.'

Activity 4   Explanation/focus exercise

- Recap simple and compound sentences. Explain that there is another type of sentence that is used to stop writing becoming boring. It is called a COMPLEX SENTENCE.
- Complex sentences are made up of CLAUSES. Explain to the students that before they start to look at complex sentences the group needs to explore clauses.
- Give out copies of Handout 72, 'What is a clause? and go through it with the students. Ask them to do the activity at the bottom of the sheet.

- Now that you have examined clauses with the students they are ready to move on to complex sentences. Give out copies of Handout 73, 'Complex sentences' and ask the students to have a go at writing and then adding detail to a complex sentence, as requested on the sheet. Check the students' work once they have all finished.

Activity 5   Focus exercise

Students should work in pairs for this activity. Give each pair one of the envelopes containing cut up text, which you prepared before the start of the session. Explain that each envelope contains a mixture of simple and compound sentences from a single text. You want them to make the sentences into complex sentences to form a shorter text, but still retaining its original meaning. They should write their finished text on a blank sheet of flipchart.

When everyone has finished the activity give each pair the chance to read out their shortened text to the rest of the group.

Activity 6   Focus exercise

For a final activity, ask students individually to pick one sentence they wrote from the pronouns exercise in Activity 2 (Handout 71). Tell them that you would now like them to write a paragraph around that sentence. They should use simple, compound and complex sentences and make sure that anything they write is grammatically correct. Take this in for marking at the end of the session so that you can judge levels of understanding.

Ww/L2.1

More prefixes and suffixes

REMINDER

- *Prefixes* are added to the *beginning* of a root word to change it.
- *Suffixes* are added to the *end* of a root word to change it.

Here are some more prefixes and an example of where they can be used:

auto   as in **auto**biography

bi   as in **bi**annual

trans   as in **trans**fixed

tele   as in **tele**vision

circum   as in **circum**stance

REMINDER

There are *rules* for adding prefixes and suffixes!

In addition, here's one more suffix and an example of where it's used:

cian as in paediatri**cian**

Can you add two more examples to each prefix and suffix?

Have you noticed that when you say some of the words, some vowels are not pronounced? For example, when you say 'television' you do not pronounce the second *i*, and when you say 'paediatrician' you do not pronounce the first *a*. These are called *unstressed vowels*.

Look out for them!

Ww/
L2.1, 2
Ws/
L2.2, 3

HANDOUT 71

More about pronouns

Remember pronouns? They are words used to replace nouns in sentences so that your writing is not repetitive.

- When Sobia got tired Sobia had a rest.
- When Sobia got tired she had a rest.

Which word is the pronoun?

There are a few types of pronouns:

POSSESSIVE PRONOUNS – used to refer to ownership, e.g. his/hers, mine/yours.

PERSONAL PRONOUNS – used when referring to a person or people directly e.g. she/he, we/us.

INDEFINITE PRONOUNS – which as their name would suggest are used to refer to something vague, e.g. anything/nobody.

INTERROGATIVE PRONOUNS – used when referring to questions, e.g. whose/which?

ACTIVITIES

1. Can you think of any more for each group?
2. Write a sentence for each type of pronoun.

Word games

1 Make a list of five words using each of the new prefixes and suffixes you have learnt in this session.

2 Make a list of ten words ending in 'ly'. Give them to someone else to identify the root word in each.

3 Each of the following boxes contains one or more sentences. The missing words in each box are HOMOPHONES. Can you fill them in?

> • Three, two, ..., BLAST OFF!
> • She .... gold at the Olympics.

> • Do you think it will .... today?
> • The Golden Jubilee celebrated 60 years of the Queen's ....
> • You use a .... to 'steer' a horse.

> • These two are a matching ....
> • This one is a juicy ....

> • This building .... is not a pretty ....

> • .... '...... coming here from over ....

4 Spot the unstressed vowel in the words below . Watch out – not all of them have one!!

station　　rested　　**general**

anaemic　　*quiet*

embrace　　spaced　　**ourselves**　　embarrass

interested　　reference

HANDOUT 72

What is a clause?

✓ A clause is a bit like a simple sentence. It is a group of words containing a verb. It does not begin with a capital letter and it does not end with a full stop. Every clause contains a verb.

✓ There are two types of clause – main clause and subordinate clause. Their titles are a good clue as to their importance:

MAIN CLAUSE

The main clause in a complex sentence is the most important one. It is the main idea in the sentence, makes complete sense on its own and could be a sentence.

SUBORDINATE CLAUSE

The subordinate clause gives more detail and information about the main clause. It would not make sense on its own! A subordinate clause can come anywhere in a sentence.

Clauses are varied and they add lots of detail and information to sentences. That is why complex sentences (which contain clauses) can make your writing more lively and interesting.

Here's an example:

The children are excited, knowing *they are having a party at playgroup.*
(main clause)   *(subordinate clause)*

Can you see the verb in each clause?

ACTIVITY

Identify the main and subordinate clause in the two sentences below.

1. Newborn babies can only be given breast or formula milk, as their stomachs cannot tolerate anything else.
2. To develop fine manipulative skills, children should be encouraged to use pencils and crayons.

Complex sentences

* Complex sentences have a varied structure, which makes them useful for livening up your writing.
* They are not suitable for all types of text writing, for example you would not use them to write a set of directions as they could make it complicated.
* As with simple and compound sentences, they do have to make grammatical sense.

Let's have a closer look at complex sentences!

A *complex sentence* is made up of more than one clause. It has one main clause and one or more supporting – or subordinate – clauses. (You looked at clauses in the last activity.)

Activity 1

Try writing a complex sentence, containing a main clause and one subordinate about any of the following:

* Something that happened in a TV programme you watched or in a book you read.
* Something you did at placement.
* Something from a story you have read to the children at placement.

Identify the two different clauses.

Remember the sentence used when we looked at clauses?

> *The children are excited, knowing they are having a party at playgroup.*

If we add another clause it gives us more information about why the children are excited:

> *The children are excited, knowing they are having a party at playgroup and <u>a magician is coming</u>.*

You could also add another clause:

> *The children are excited, knowing they are having a party at playgroup and a magician is coming <u>to show them some magic tricks</u>.*

Activity 2

Try doing this with your original complex sentence. How much detail could you add to it while using correct grammar and punctuation?

SESSION 2

Outline

Punctuation is the main focus of Session 2. As well as exploring some new kinds with the students, the object of this session is to analyse the use and purpose of them in reading and writing.

For this session you will need:

- Photocopied passages from fictional texts or magazines (each passage should be at least five paragraphs long). Make sure there is some speech in the text and a variety of punctuation marks. (Children's fiction is good for this activity.) Make sure that the title of the book or article is not shown!
- A selection of newspapers – tabloid, broadsheet and financial.

Activities

Activity 1 Introduction

- Recap punctuation marks that students know and can use.
- Give out copies of Handout 74, 'Punctuation marks and their uses' and remind students of the different sorts and their functions. (Students will know some of these already, but it is useful revision.)

Rs/L2.2
SLd/L
2.2, 4

- Give out the photocopied texts you collected before the session started and tell students to read through the piece you have given them. Ask them to identify all punctuation marks and make notes about what they have been used for.
- Discuss findings as a whole class.
- Finish off by handing out Activity Sheet 59, 'Punctuate these sentences' and ask the group to go through the sheet, punctuating all eight sentences.

Activity 2 Explanation/paired discussion

Explain to the learners that when we read we often get a feel for how an article has been approached and written. It is usually clear when a subject has been taken seriously or has been dealt with in a 'tongue in cheek' way, and very often we can sense when something has been written with belief.

We can all tell this by looking at many things in a text. Give out copies of Handout 75, 'Meaning and purpose' and read through the various clues that 'signal' to us as we read. Looking again at the text used in the last activity, ask students to read the text in pairs and individually to make some notes using Handout 76, 'What am I reading?'. The students should then discuss the text with their partner.

Activity 3 Focus exercise

Recap skimming and scanning from previous levels and then arrange the group into pairs. Start by giving each pair a tabloid and a broadsheet with at least two articles that appear in both papers. Tell the students that you want them to compare the articles as they appear in each paper, using the following points as a guide:

- Where is it in the paper?
- Where is it on the page?
- Layout of the article
- Level of formality
- Use of pictures, images, etc.
- Level of information/detail
- Vocabulary and language use
- Sentence structure
- Conclusions, questions, etc.
- How the article ends
- Any ambiguity or contradiction
- Level of objectivity.

Encourage the students to discuss the findings in their pairs and to make notes as they study the articles together.

As a further extension to this exercise, join pairs together to make small groups of four. Each pair is to tell the other pair what they have found out about each of their articles. They should start by discussing what it was about and what its purpose was.

Rs/L2.2

HANDOUT 74

Punctuation marks and their uses

	NAME	WHEN TO USE IT	EXAMPLE
.	Full stop	To end a sentence	We have reached the end.
,	Comma	To make smaller breaks within a sentence; to separate some parts of sentences	I have seen that film, but I didn't like it much.
!	Exclamation mark	To indicate strong feeling, e.g. anger, surprise	Shut up!
?	Question mark	To end a sentence that is asking a question	When shall we do this?
;	Semi-colon	To make a break in a sentence	I waited; nothing happened.
:	Colon	Before a list	The following things can be used:
—	Dash	To quickly add information that is relevant to the rest of the sentence	– I know it sounds strange –
( )	Brackets	To add information that is not relevant to the sentence	(I know it sounds strange)
-	Hyphen	To join two words to make a new one	Multi-lingual
'	Apostrophe	To show something belongs to someone or something has been missed out	June's book. Isn't it?
...	Ellipsis	To show something is unfinished	Her voice softened ...
' '	Inverted commas	To show something is being referred to by name	This 'thingee'
" "	Speech marks	To show when someone is speaking	"Hello", said the man.
<u>cat</u>	Underlining	To emphasise something or for titles and sub-titles	<u>The Story of Me</u>

Punctuate these sentences

1 would you like me to come in with you

2 to work as a team you need to understand
   the roles of those you work with

3 examples of objects you can use are
   wooden spoons
   cones
   shells
   natural sponges

4 this book is jackies

5 we study the stages and sequences of children's
   development

6 babies can be given any type of object
   that is safe for them to touch hold and put
   in their mouths

7 tell you what he said feigning innocence

8 gail showed the students how to bath a
   baby then watched them do it

Rt/L2.1
Rw/
L2.1, 3

HANDOUT 75

Meaning and purpose

There are so many different newspapers, aren't there? Each with its own style, 'agenda', political allegiance, etc. All this variety makes for interesting reading, however, and depending on what you are interested in it will influence which one you buy. For example, if you were interested in Robbie Williams' latest escapade you wouldn't read the Financial Times! If you wanted to check your stocks and shares you wouldn't go for the Sun!

There are lots of clues that give us a feel for the purpose of text and its level of seriousness:

- Types of words used – are they serious, humorous, technical, etc.?
- Level of detail – is there a lot of detail or on closer inspection not much there?
- Is it grammatically correct or is it written with a touch of slang?
- Use of abstract nouns, the third person and passive verbs can signal the level of formality in a text.
- Are the words used a particular type, for example are they words to persuade or confuse?
- 'Argumentative' or 'provocative' language.
- Repetitive language or rhetorical questions.
- Is there use of ambiguity?
- How is it set out – in structured paragraphs, short sharp paragraphs and sentences?

All of these can signal to you – along with pictures, graphics and so on – to help you judge the meaning of text.

HANDOUT 76

What am I reading?

Read the text you used earlier on in detail and make some notes to enable you to discuss it with your partner. Ask yourself the following questions as you read through the text:

- What is the purpose of this text?

- Where could it have come from?

- Who is it written for?

- What type of language does it use?

- What is the topic or subject of this text?

- What are the main points?

- What is the specific detail that supports the main point?

- How can you tell the main points from the detail?

SESSION 3

Outline

Here the students have the opportunity to examine the purposes of different sorts of text and then to share with the group their own understanding and opinions about what the writer was hoping to achieve.

For this session you will need:

- A selection of different types of letters, leaflets, circulars, prospectuses, short stories, photocopied extracts from textbooks and magazines. You will need enough for students to have one of each while working in pairs.
- Some photocopied text from a child development theory (Piaget is good for this activity), which must be at least five paragraphs long. You will need one copy for each student.

Activities

Activity 1 Introduction

- Begin this session by recapping work done on meaning and purpose in the last session. Can students recall what they were looking for, what points they had to find while reading, etc.? Explain that all texts have a purpose and will be written and set out to suit that purpose.
- Arrange students into pairs for the first activity. Give each pair a wide selection of leaflets, photocopied extracts, etc. along with a copy of Activity Sheet 60, 'Statements of purpose'. Ask them to identify the purposes of the texts you have given them, following the instructions on the sheet.

SLc/L2.1, 2, 3, 4
- Students should then share their findings in a paired or whole-class discussion. This will give you an opportunity to check the work they have just done.

Activity 2 Explanation

Rt/L2.1, 2, 3, 8
Explain that when we read we do not just look at the words on a page, we make sense of what we are reading. As an instant example of what you mean give out copies of Handout 77, 'Reading text' and go through it with the students. The skills and knowledge mentioned on the sheet are precisely the ones helping them to make sense of the text on the handout!

Activity 3 Discussion

This activity starts with an individual reading exercise which then forms the basis of a paired or small group discussion. Give each student a copy of Handout 78, 'Lynsey's text'. Point out that this text was written by a CACHE DCE student for a course assignment. Ask students to read the text and make notes based on the following points:

- What are the main points in this writing?
- Identify the detail that supports the main points.

- What is the purpose of this text?
- Are there any main points that are enough on their own, i.e. get the point across without any detail?
- What is the overall message from this text?

Once they have completed their detailed examination of the text, ask the students to discuss what they have found out in pairs or small groups.

SLd/L2.1, 2, 3, 4, 5

Activity 4 Idea storm/focus exercise

Wt/L2.1, 2, 3, 6
Rt/L2.1, 2, 8

Give each student a copy of the text you photocopied from the child development theory before the start of the session. Tell them that you want them individually to read it in detail and write a summary of the text. Explain that the summary will be taken in for marking along with any plans, drafts, etc. that they have made during the exercise.

Kick off with an idea storm of what they need to do to write the summary. The group should ask themselves the following questions:

- Who or what is this summary for?
- What must go into it?
- What might go into it?
- How long should it be?
- How much detail does it need to contain?
- What type of language should be used?
- How should it be structured?
- How should paragraphs be sequenced?

With the idea storm over, students should spend the rest of the session rereading the piece of informative writing they were given at the start of the session, making notes and planning their writing.

Take their summaries in for marking at the end of the session.

ACTIVITY SHEET 60

Statements of purpose

Listed in the table below are some different purposes of text.

- Skim through the leaflets, letters and other texts you have been given and decide which of the purposes below applies to each of them.
- List the text types under the appropriate heading in the table and consider whether the purpose was explicit or implicit.

Now read the texts more carefully:

- Was the purpose different to what you thought it was when you skimmed through the text? Give reasons for your decision, e.g. layout, language, etc.

To give a personal opinion	To make you laugh	To explain a process or give information using objectivity	To persuade you about something

To present an argument for or against	To complain	To justify something	Other

Reading text

When we read we don't just look at words, we use other skills and knowledge to help us make sense of what we are reading.

Skills and knowledge we use:

✓ Knowledge of words and what they mean

✓ Knowledge of different sentence types and their uses

✓ Knowledge of the different parts of speech; when they are used and what for

✓ Different reading skills: skimming, scanning and detailed reading

✓ Types of words and when we are likely to see them being used

✓ Recognition of the layout/format of different text types

✓ Knowledge of different language types and when they are used.

We will also consider the following questions:

❏ Is this relevant to my needs?

❏ Do I need to read this?

❏ Do I want to read this? (Don't forget we read for pleasure too – we all need a bit of escapism now and again!)

❏ Is this valid? Is it based on truth and backed up with detail/examples?

❏ Is this objective, persuasive or 'tongue-in-cheek'?

❏ How good is it?

HANDOUT 78

Lynsey's text

What is Lynsey writing about and why?

The cultural aspirations of the parent on the child may change the way in which some children are involved within the setting. Some parents, due to religious or cultural reasons, may prefer that their child doesn't participate in some things that go on in the daily routine of the primary setting. Parents should not be challenged on this or made to feel they are in the wrong especially if they hold very strong beliefs, in the culture or religion which they follow. These aspirations may be to do with the child's diet, daily activities or clothing and the parent must be kept informed about what is going on and the child's involvement in the daily routine of the setting.

The child may begin to feel different from the other children in the class because of these reasons. It is the early years worker who must reassure both the concerned child and others that difference is not negative and pursue it in a positive way. Different cultures and a multi-cultural environment allow a wider perspective and enriches all those involved. It allows the children to have a sense of identity and a sense of being valued. It also promotes awareness of others and celebrates similarities and differences; it promotes respect and tolerance among the group, including discussion.

Children are able to gain self-awareness and it encourages self-belief and values. The children can see equality and diversity and these positive points will balance out the perceived 'negative' aspects.

Reproduced by kind permission of Lynsey Brogan
(First year CACHE DCE student)
South Birmingham College
Early Years Department
July 2002

Outline

The next three sessions are all based on a course assignment in which students are asked to research and write an essay on children's language development. As the whole process is relatively time-consuming the task has been broken down into three parts, each designed to fit into a single session. It is also advised that you set aside half an hour at the end of a session for private reading or word games/activities such as Scrabble. Many students will find the assignment heavy going, and including some light-hearted activities will help maintain higher concentration and interest levels.

Session 4 gives students the opportunity to revise the skim, scan and detailed reading techniques covered in previous levels and to explore sequences within persuasive and descriptive writing. Before being introduced to the assignment itself, Part One of which involves using the library to research information for the essay, the students have a chance to familiarise themselves with the library.

For this session you will need:

- Use of the library.
- Highlighter pens.
- Photocopier access for students.

Activities

Activity 1 Introduction

Get the session under way by recapping reading skills and the different approaches we can take when we read, e.g. skimming, scanning and detailed reading. (As a reminder you could let the students have another look at Handout 45, 'Reading' from Entry Level Three (p. 160).)

Activity 2 Explanation/focus exercise

Give out copies of Handout 79, 'Sequencing writing' and go through it with the students. Ask them to do the activity at the bottom of the sheet. The exercise should help them when it comes to thinking about how to sequence their writing in the forthcoming assignment.

Activity 3 Explanation

- Move on to discuss students' experience of libraries. Have any of them ever visited or joined a library?
- Give out copies of Handout 80, 'The library' and read through it with the students. Following this, distribute copies of Handout 81, 'How to use the library' and explain to the group how easy it is to find information once you know your way around a library!
- Take students on a tour of the library in your setting or, alternatively, organise a trip to the local library.

Activity 4   Explanation

Now it's time to introduce the assignment to the students. Give each learner a copy of Activity Sheet 61, 'Assignment!' and read through it together, exploring the various stages of the task as you look through the sheet.

Reassure them that while it looks like a mammoth task, the whole thing doesn't have to be completed today! Explain that they will be concentrating on a few steps at a time over the next few sessions.

Tell the students that in today's session you want them to complete Part One of the assignment, i.e. Steps 1 and 2. The focus will be on finding information for the task ahead, applying their knowledge of how to use the library.

Sequencing writing

When thinking about how to sequence your writing, you must consider the PURPOSE, CONTENT and your AUDIENCE. Let's look at two common types of text: *persuasive* and *explanatory or descriptive*.

Persuasive text

In this type of text you are trying to convince the reader about something.

Example:

You have been asked by your tutor to write an essay on 'The importance of bonding and attachment'. You will need to sequence your writing in a way that will convince your tutor about what you have learnt. Here's a good way to approach it:

Paragraph 1

Introduce the topic with some supporting detail – not too much. Remember this is the introduction.

It is essential that new-born babies be given contact with their primary carers, as soon as they are born, in order for the bonding process to begin etc.

Paragraph 2

Explain the bonding process and forming of attachments etc.

Paragraph 3

Explain why this needs to happen and give evidence of research: Bowlby's theory of attachment etc.

Paragraph 4

Conclude with words that support your opening statement and perhaps a concluding thought from you. In coursework, tutors like to see that students are able to think and evaluate for themselves.

HANDOUT 79 continued

Explanatory or descriptive text

In this type of text you could be explaining how or why something has happened. You need to consider how much information the reader needs about the event before you go into explaining what or how something happened.

Example:

Following a minor accident at placement you have been asked to write a report. Here's a good way to approach it:

Paragraph 1

Start by setting the scene:

On Thursday 9th June the children were playing outside in the play area. This is a sectioned off area of the playground specifically for use by the nursery children. There was a selection of bikes, cars and prams for them to play with. There were twelve children in the play area.

Paragraph 2

Explain what you saw happen, how it happened and who was involved.

Paragraph 3

Describe what you did, what happened after that, and so on.

Using persuasive and explanatory text together

In some cases you may need to use both techniques in your writing at the same time.

Example:

You are writing to parents to ask for help with fund raising for something. Here's a good way to approach it:

Paragraph 1

Explain to parents what you want and why.

Paragraph 2

Try to persuade the parents to help by telling them about the benefits to the children and the enjoyment they will get from it.

Paragraph 3

Explain how much money you need to raise and encourage parents to help you raise it.

ACTIVITY

You want to raise money for some outdoor play equipment.
Try writing a letter to parents/carers of children who attend a local playgroup. The playgroup is voluntary – it receives no funding apart from the fees of children attending.

The library

If you looked in a dictionary you might see 'library' defined as a collection of books or records, which is quite right.

When we think of a library, we usually think of a building or a room full of different types of books that people borrow and use, or somewhere people go to work quietly.

Libraries (is 'libraries' singular or plural?) are not only full of books that people can borrow. They have reference sections where you can go and look up information, and magazines, newspapers (old and current), journals and computers with access to the Internet.

The books, magazines and journals you see will be written by lots of different people and set out in a wide variety of formats, sizes and text types.

Having all this in one place means that the library has got to be well organised:

- Books of the same category are kept together in sections.
- They are shelved in a system by author and number.
- Records of all the items in the library are kept on computer so that staff can easily answer people's queries.

The library is organised in this way so that:

- You know where to look for a type of book.
- You can find specific books easily if you know the author.
- Books are easy to put back in the right place.
- It is easy to access information if you need help finding something.
- It saves you time!

Rt/L2.6

HANDOUT 81

How to use the library

This is how books will usually be organised in the library:

- By topic or subject section, e.g. Childcare
- By sub-topic, e.g. Child development
- By author – arranged alphabetically by surname, e.g. Smith, Maureen
- Each book will have a code number on the spine as well as the title and the author's name. This makes it easy to skim/scan to find the book you want.

Once you have found the books you want:

- You take them to the librarian
- The librarian books them out to you, stamps them with the date they are due back by and scans them (so the alarms don't go off when you leave!).

FINDING THE INFORMATION YOU NEED

Here are some guidelines for finding the information you need when you get to the library.

Step 1
Decide what you are looking for. If necessary make a list or some notes before you go. Imagine you are looking for information about children's language development.

Step 2
Go to the relevant section in the library, e.g. Childcare.

Step 3
Locate books on child development. Skim the titles and authors and choose two books to start with.

Step 4
Scan the index of each book and make a list of pages that might have useful information on them.

Step 5
Go through the pages chosen and scan the texts. If you think they are useful or relevant photocopy them.

Step 6
Read, in detail, the photocopied pages you have chosen and highlight or underline any paragraphs, sentences, phrases or words that are useful to you.

Step 7
Put the information into note form (spidergram, list, notes), ready to use when you are planning your work.

ACTIVITY SHEET 61

Assignment!

> ✳ For a course assignment you have to research and write an essay on children's language development.
>
> ✳ The assignment is in three parts. Each part is divided into two or more steps and guidelines have been given to help you complete each one.

Part One

STEP 1

`Rt/L2.6, 7`

✳ Find two theories about how children develop their language skills. Search for them using what you have learnt about libraries and finding information. Have another read of 'Finding the information you need' on Handout 81 and follow the guidelines provided.

✳ When you have found your two theories, write a step-by-step account of how you tracked down the information. Read and summarise the two theories.

STEP 2

`Rt/L2.7, 8 Rw/ L2.1, 3`

✳ Look carefully through the text you photocopied in Step 1 and highlight or underline the information you think will be useful for your essay. Remember, you need to identify main points and supporting detail.

✳ Write down why you chose these particular pieces of text.

Part Two

STEP 3

`Wt/ L2.1, 4`

✳ Now have a closer look at the information you have collected.

✳ Make an initial plan (using notes and/or diagrams) of what bit of information you would like to include in your essay, the audience you will be writing for and the purpose of your writing.

ACTIVITY SHEET 61 continued

STEP 4
* Decide what bits of information MUST be included. Think about what you need to consider when making such a decision
* Make a decision about how long your piece of writing will be.

STEP 5
* Now plan your essay.
* Think about what will go where, what the first paragraph will be about, how many paragraphs will there be in total?
* When you have done this spend some time thinking about what you needed to consider while you were planning your essay.

Part Three

STEP 6
* Make the first draft. Don't forget to think about language style, amount of detail, format, etc.
* When your first draft is complete, make short notes about how you did it.

STEP 7
* Proof-read and edit your draft. You may have to do this more than once!

STEP 8
* When you have completed your editing and are happy with your drafting, write out a final copy of your essay.
* Remember to consider all you have learnt about spelling, punctuation and grammar.
* Hand in your planning, draft and final piece of writing to your tutor for marking.

YOU HAVE DONE IT!
WELL DONE!

SESSION 5

Outline

As explained previously, this session is a continuation of the last session where students researched some information for an essay writing task. The concentration in this session will be on Part Two of the assignment and learners will need to start by looking at their copies of Activity Sheet 61, 'Assignment!'

Activities

Activity 1 | Introduction

Recap the library work that students did in the last session. Did they find it easy to find the information they were asked to look for? Was there a lot to sift through? Did they find the skim/scan techniques useful?

Activity 2 | Focus exercise

- Explain to the students that you would like them to complete Part Two of the assignment, i.e. Steps 3, 4 and 5 in this session.
- Ask them to start by reading through these sections on Activity Sheet 61 and explain that now they have done the research for their assignment they need to decide what bits of information they are going to include in their essay.
- The final stage of Part Two is to plan the essay in note or diagrammatic form.

SESSION 6

Outline

The object of this session is for students to complete the assignment they have been working on for the last two sessions.

Activities

Activity 1   Introduction

As usual, start by recapping what the students did last session and discuss how members of the group feel they are getting on. How far did they get last time? Are they finding the steps easy to follow and complete? Identify any areas that are causing problems and, if possible, consider extending the time allocated for the assignment if it looks as though students might need longer to complete the essay.

Activity 2   Focus exercise

Students should take out their copies of Activity Sheet 61, 'Assignment!' and read through Part Three. Ask them to continue with Steps 6 and 7. If they finish drafting and checking their essay they can then go on to attempt Step 8. If they run out of time, the final step can be done as homework or you might wish to spend another session on it.

➤ Researching, planning, drafting and writing an essay is a monumental achievement for most, if not all, of your students. On reaching the end of the assignment they deserve an enormous amount of praise and congratulations.

SESSION 7

Outline

This session is an IT session. Students will be using their skills to access and use information from the World Wide Web.

> For this session you will need:
>
> • Computer access for students working together in pairs.

Activities

Activity 1   Introduction

- To start with make the point that sometimes we read and see arguments about different topics. Explain to the group that by 'argument' you don't mean the 'fisticuffs' sort where those involved have a hostile disagreement. Instead you mean an exchange of views in which different sides of an argument are put across. The differing points of view will be put forward by two or more parties and you will be left to decide who you agree with.
- Give out copies of Handout 82, 'Presenting an argument' and go through the points at the top of the sheet before asking the students to read the excerpt from the *Guardian* dated 21 January 2003. Discuss what is being said in this article, how the two sides of the argument are presented, and what the different points of view are.

Activity 2   Explanation/focus exercise

- Divide students into pairs or small groups. Check that they are comfortable with using a computer. Make sure those who are not have access to support.
- Explain that you want students to search the World Wide Web for some points of view on particular topics. You will give them a number of different options and they will be able to choose which one they want to explore. Point out that the aim of this activity is to look at different arguments from a variety of sources and to examine the way they are set out.
- Write the following on the flipchart and ask the pairs/small groups to choose one of the topics to research:

  - Immunisation – the for and against argument.
  - Influence of TV violence on children – does it or doesn't it?
  - Smacking children – should we or shouldn't we?

- Set students off on their Internet search. They may need some help with finding sites/search engines. Encourage them to print off information as and when they find it.
- When everyone has found a selection of arguments on their chosen topic, give out copies of Activity Sheet 62, 'The argument is...' and ask students to work through the sheet in relation to the articles/information they have found on the Web. Explain that point 6 on the handout will be carried out during the next session, so once students have completed points 1–5 they should use the rest of this session to prepare for the discussion.

Rt/L2.4

HANDOUT 82

Presenting an argument

When you read an article that is presenting an 'argument' you should see the following characteristics:

✳ The article usually opens with some background/information about the issue followed by presentation of both points of view.
✳ The positives/negatives and opinions for/against will be presented.
✳ People on both sides of the argument will present their own point of view.
✳ Vocabulary used will be factual and objective.
✳ Words and phrases will be specific to the argument.
✳ You might see expressions of personal feeling being used to persuade you to agree with a particular point of view.

'Battle over grammar schools re-ignited'
by Rebecca Smithers (Education correspondent)

The battle to end educational selection through the 11-plus was re-ignited yesterday, as the education secretary, Charles Clarke, called for a debate on the impact of grammar schools on standards.

He spoke as the first major push to scrap selection since Labour came to power in 1997 was launched with the backing of former cabinet minister Frank Dobson. In his interview with the Guardian, Mr Clarke insisted he did not want to "kill off" the 164 surviving grammar schools in England by changing the law, but left the door open to further discussion.

He spoke as Labour MPs, party members, academics, and parents were being urged to back the new campaign to end selection, which if successful could lead to a formal change to Labour policy by 2004.

Campaigners warn that partial selection is likely to increase as a result of Labour's expansion of its specialist schools programme, where schools are allowed to select up to 10% of their pupils by aptitude.

Mr Clarke denied specialist schools led to selection by postcode and pointed out new regulations curbing the ability of faith schools to select by interview: "Some 98% of specialist schools do not have selection," he said, adding: "We have just passed a regulation on church schools saying they can no longer interview in that way."

Mr Dobson said selection was socially and educationally divisive. Asked about reports that Mr Clarke was "secretly backing" the campaign, he said: "If so, it's being kept secret from me."

Taken from the *Guardian*
21 January 2003

© June Green (2003) *Basic Skills for Childcare – Literacy*. Published by David Fulton Publishers Ltd.

The argument is . . .

You have printed off some 'arguments' for and against specific issues, from the World Wide Web. Now look at the points below and write your responses on a separate sheet of paper.

1. What is your chosen argument about?

2. What are the main points being made for each side of the argument?

3. Who is making the points for and who is making the points against? This could be a group of people, an organisation or an individual.

4. Highlight words that are specific to the argument. Make a list of any that are unfamiliar to you.

5. Cut up the article you have printed off and think about how you would use the main points to present your own view about this issue in a discussion.

6. You will be expected to take part in a discussion about the issue next session so keep the work you've done safe. You will be asked to give your point of view and support it with evidence/detail.

SESSION 8

Outline

The main focus of this session is the group discussion mentioned at the end of Session 7.

> For this session you will need:
>
> • Students' written responses to the questions and instructions on Activity Sheet 62.

Activities

Activity 1 Introduction

Start off with a group discussion about what students did in the last session. How did the learners get on? What skills did they use? Did they find it easy to access information on the Internet?

Activity 2 Small group discussion

Explain to the students that they will be working in small groups for this activity. They will be discussing the arguments they found on the Web during Session 7, presenting their points of view on the issues they chose. Give them a short time to think about:

• How they will express themselves
• Vocabulary they might use
• How they will show they are listening to others
• How they will respond if they are asked questions or disagree with someone
• Their body language.

Ask the students to begin discussing the issues within their groups. It is up to you how long you let this activity go on for. Some groups will have lots to say and others might be a bit more reticent!

Activity 3 Reflection

For the rest of the session do some 'fun' oral quizzes or games to revise the work done in the previous sessions. Alternatively, let students do some quiet reading on their own.

SESSION 9

Outline

The object of this final session is to introduce the last bits of punctuation and parts of speech that students have not yet dealt with. As well as building on previous dictionary work, students will also be introduced to another important source of words and phrases – the thesaurus.

For this session you will need:

- Enough dictionaries (preferably not all the same kind) and thesauruses for each student to work from individually during this session.
- The words *similes*, *metaphors*, *idioms* and *clichés*, each written on a separate sheet of flipchart.
- A selection of children's verse and some short poems.
- A range of texts containing inverted commas, speech marks, semi-colons, colons and dashes.
- Different coloured highlighter pens.
- Copies of Handout 74, 'Punctuation marks and their uses' from Session 2 (p. 248).

Activities

Activity 1   Introduction

- Recap use and structure of dictionaries, which students first covered in Session 5 of Entry Level Two. Explain that another excellent source of words and references is a THESAURUS – a book containing lists of synonyms (ask students to look up 'synonym' in their dictionaries).
- Give out copies of Handout 83, 'What can we use a thesaurus for?' and go through it with the students. Discuss the example of an entry from the thesaurus given at the bottom of the sheet. Point out that it's a list of various types of words, all of which could have different uses – some would be suitable in certain contexts but not in others.
- Explain that they express both different and related things: in part 1, for example, the words are to do with growth and change; in part 2 the words are about happenings and events. Nevertheless, they could all be used in place of the word 'development'.
- Give each student a copy of Activity Sheet 63, 'Using a thesaurus' and ask them to complete the exercise individually.
- Discuss answers once everyone has finished the activity. (Some possible answers have been provided for you in Figure 6.1.)

Activity 2   Explanation/focus exercise

- Explain to students that there are some other sorts of words that they need to know and use. These are: similes, metaphors, idioms and clichés.
- Display flipcharts around the room with these four words written on them. Divide the students into four groups and give each group one of the words from the flipchart. Ask

Tutor's answers to 'Using a thesaurus' activity

1. This activity <u>gives</u> the children the chance to learn about shapes.
2. To develop and <u>grow</u>, children need to receive nutrients from a variety of foods.
3. Babies <u>need</u> attention in the first few months of life.
4. Sheila <u>visits</u> all the students at placement and keeps a record of their progress.
5. When children start school their personal information is kept in their <u>records</u>, which are stored safely.
6. Students will learn about children's growth and <u>development</u> while <u>training</u>.

Figure 6.1 Answers to exercises on Activity Sheet 63

them to first find the meaning of their word in a dictionary. Can they find the word in a thesaurus? What other words could be used in the place of the ones they have been given?

- Discuss results of the activity together.

Activity 3 Focus exercise

As an extension to Activity 2, give out the poems and children's verse you collected before the start of the session. Ask the students to read through them to see if they can find any similes, metaphors, idioms and clichés.

Ws/L2.4 Activity 4 Explanation/focus exercise

- Using Handout 74, 'Punctuation marks and their uses' from Session 2 (p. 248) recap inverted commas, speech marks, semi-colons, colons and dashes.
- Give out the texts containing these sorts of punctuation marks and ask the students to highlight each type in a different colour, list them and explain their uses.
- Now ask students to write some sentences incorporating these punctuation marks. At the end of the exercise they should explain which ones they have used and what the different marks have been used for.

Activity 5 Focus exercise

End the session with a lively 'synonyms' quiz. Arrange students into teams and see which team can think up the most synonyms for these words:

- Speaking
- Listening.

What can we use a thesaurus for?

A thesaurus is a book that lists synonyms. Synonyms are words that have the same or very similar meanings to others.

A thesaurus helps us to avoid repetition in our writing by suggesting alternative words.

A thesaurus can be used to find:

- a word that is more definite
- a word that is more formal (or informal)
- a more vivid word for describing something
- a more simple word to explain something
- the right word when you just can't think of it
- an alternative word when you are just plain bored with using the same old one!

A thesaurus is organised in much the same way as a dictionary. Under the heading of the main word, the synonyms are often listed in alphabetical order.

Here's an example of an entry:

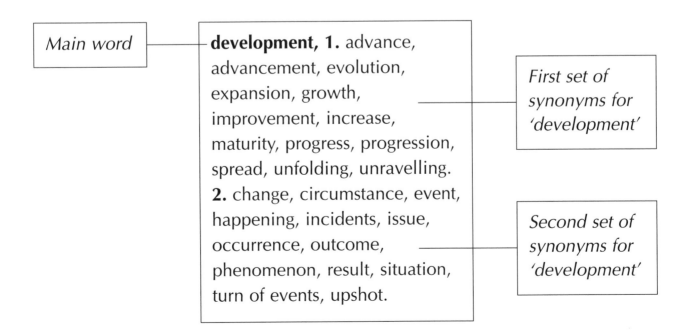

Main word

development, 1. advance, advancement, evolution, expansion, growth, improvement, increase, maturity, progress, progression, spread, unfolding, unravelling. **2.** change, circumstance, event, happening, incidents, issue, occurrence, outcome, phenomenon, result, situation, turn of events, upshot.

First set of synonyms for 'development'

Second set of synonyms for 'development'

ACTIVITY SHEET 63

Using a thesaurus

Have a look at the sentences below.

They have a word underlined that could be replaced to make the sentence sound better. Use a thesaurus to find a synonym to improve the sentence.

1. This activity <u>allows</u> the children the chance to learn about shapes.
2. To develop and <u>enlarge</u>, children need to receive nutrients from a variety of foods.
3. Babies <u>crave</u> attention in the first few months of life.

The following sentences need some words adding to them. Use a thesaurus to find a word that fits the context and structure of the sentence. Try a few words out and see which one sounds best.

4. Sheila . . . . all the students at placement and keeps a record of their progress.
5. When children start school their personal information is kept in their . . . ., which are stored safely.
6. Students will learn about children's growth and . . . . while . . . .

Speaking and Listening activities for Level Two

For these activities you will need:

- A couple of taped stories of different types for students to listen to as a group.
- A couple of other short stories to read to students.
- Four people with different jobs from outside the setting, to take part in a quiz, e.g. fireman, nurse, bookseller, etc.

Activity 1

SLc/ L2.1, 3, 4

Students will each need to give a five-minute talk on a topic of their choice, using a visual aid.

➤ Students should be given a week to prepare for this.

Activity 2

SLd/L2.1, 2, 3, 4, 5

Prepare for a group discussion by agreeing on a topic as a whole class. The group should begin by idea storming subjects that they would like to discuss and as they make suggestions list these on the flipchart. Remove those topics that any of them feel they could not discuss. Once you are left with two or three topics take a vote on which one the group would like to discuss. The majority wins!

➤ Again the students will need time to prepare for the discussion, as everyone will be expected to take part.

Activity 3

SLlr/L2.1 SLc/ L2.1, 2

Arrange a time when it is convenient for all four of your visitors to come to the setting to take part in a quiz. The object of this quiz is for students to find out, through questioning, what jobs the four people do. They should use a variety of questions and listen carefully to the responses.

Activity 4

SLlr/ L2.2, 3

Students should listen to the taped and read stories. They should then discuss how each one built up to the ending. Did the students need to listen to every word in each story to find out what was going on? Ask the students questions on the stories to see how much they have managed to remember.

Activity 5

Discuss the topic of 'criticism' together as a group. Explore what it is, how it should be given, what is appropriate criticism and what is inappropriate. How might people react to it? How should they react to it? Should it be challenged? What are the dangers if it is never challenged?

Role-play a couple of situations where criticism is given and received. Observers should comment on the verbal and non-verbal language used: did they feel it was appropriate or not? How could it have been better? Were the receiver's actions justified/appropriate? How might the 'critic' have done it differently?

Conclusion

Well, that's the end of Basic Skills Literacy. You have all come a long way since Entry Level One. It's taken a lot of hard work and commitment from everyone involved – both the learners and yourself.

The students will have learnt vital skills that they will be able to use in all aspects of everyday life. As their tutor you have opened up new doors for them, helped them to gain confidence and to further their chances of employment.

What more is there to say except WELL DONE YOU!